VGM Opportunities Series

OPPORTUNITIES IN
SPORTS AND
ATHLETICS
CAREERS

Wm. Ray Heitzmann

VGM Career Horizons
a division of *NTC Publishing Group*
Lincolnwood, Illinois USA

Library of Congress Cataloging-in-Publication Data

Heitzmann, William Ray.
    Opportunities in sports and athletics careers / Wm. Ray Heitzmann.
       p.   cm. — (VGM opportunities series)
    Rev. ed. of: Opportunities in sports and athletics. c1985.
    Includes bibliographical references (p.   ).
    ISBN 0-8442-4051-6 — ISBN 0-8442-4052-4 (pbk.)
    1. Sports—Vocational guidance—United States.   I. Heitzmann,
William Ray. Opportunities in sports and athletics. II. Title.
III. Series.
GV734.H46   1993
796'.023—dc20   92-37844
                                                           CIP

Published by VGM Career Horizons, a division of NTC Publishing Group.
© 1993 by NTC Publishing Group, 4255 West Touhy Avenue,
Lincolnwood (Chicago), Illinois 60646-1975 U.S.A.
All rights reserved. No part of this book may be reproduced, stored
in a retrieval system, or transmitted in any form or by any means,
electronic, mechanical, photocopying, recording or otherwise, without
the prior permission of NTC Publishing Group.
Manufactured in the United States of America.

3 4 5 6 7 8 9 0 VP 9 8 7 6 5 4 3 2 1

ABOUT THE AUTHOR

Ray Heitzmann, a faculty member at Villanova University, has taught and coached successfully in New Jersey, Pennsylvania, Illinois, and New York at the high school and college level. Formerly he taught in the College of Allied Health Sciences at Thomas Jefferson University. His specialties in coaching include development of fundamental skills, performance enhancement, strategy and tactics, and sports literature. During the 1980s his interest in women's sports greatly expanded; the 1990s found him coaching women's AAU basketball. His flag football team won the Philadelphia area college championship and participated in the National Women's Flag Football Championship.

Ray has written a variety of articles on sports and athletics; some have appeared in *Coach and Athlete, Illinois Libraries, The Beachcomber, Coaching Clinic, Catholic Library World, PhillySport,* the *Philadelphia Inquirer,* the *National Association of Basketball Coaches Bulletin* and others. He has appeared frequently on radio and television shows discussing sports careers, academics and athletics, and sports in society.

In the area of career education he has worked with groups of school students, taught in-service courses for educators, spoken at conferences, and published articles in *Real World, Career World,* the California *Social Studies Review,* and others. His *Opportunities in Sports Medicine, Opportunities in Marine and Maritime Careers,* and *Careers for*

iii

Sports Nuts and Other Athletic Types have been published by the VGM Careers Division of NTC Publishing.

In the wonderful world of sports, in addition to playing and coaching, he has had the good fortune to serve as a sportswriter, guest commentator on professional wrestling and basketball, umpire, referee, and fan, and gladly admits loving them all.

ACKNOWLEDGMENTS

The author would like to thank the many players, coaches, and associates who have contributed to his love and knowledge of sports. In terms of this book, the author wishes to thank the following: Barry Mano, Publisher and Executive Editor, *Referee* magazine; Andy McGovern, Sports Collectible Specialist, Narberth, PA; John Robinson, Athletic Coach and Fitness Specialist, San Diego; Tim McCarver, TV sports broadcaster and commentator; Deena Shelton, cameraperson, major league baseball; Vincent DiStefano, M.D., Sports Orthopedist, Human Performance and Sports Medicine Center, Wayne, PA; Richie Philips, attorney and sports representative; Bob Lambert, sports equipment manager, Villanova University; Henry Nichols, Ed.D., NCAA National Coordinator Men's Basketball Officials; Don Casey, Assistant Coach, Boston Celtics Professional Basketball Team, NBA; Donald Davidson, statistician and historian, U.S. Auto Club; Skippy Kingwill, basketball referee, Northern New Jersey; Otho Davis, Executive Director, National Athletic Trainers Association, and head athletic trainer, Philadelphia Eagles; Jim Corea, Ph.D., R.P.T., Moorestown, NJ; Larry Hanzel, Athletic Director (Retired), North Chicago High School; James Clinkingboard, Director, Educational Affairs, American Physical Therapy Association; Mary Bielinski, Administrative Assistant, Women's Professional Bowlers Association; Stan Gallup, Executive Secretary-Treasurer, Golden Gloves Association of America; Vincent Francia,

Director of Public Relations and Marketing, Penn National Race Course; Capt. A. J. Rubino, USNR (Ret.), Deputy Physical Education Officer, U.S. Naval Academy; Janet Lippincott, physical educator, coach (retired), Springside (PA) School; Canada's Sports Hall of Fame; Ronnie Barnes, New York Giants, NFL; Don Henderson, Sports Manager, WOGL-AM Radio, Philadelphia, PA; Tony Leodora, Sports Editor, *Times—Herald,* Norristown, PA; Fr. Marty Smith, OSA, Villanova University; Laura Schiller, aerobics instructor, West Chester, PA; Dick Hall, equipment manager, USMA; Joel Goodhart, Professional Wrestling Promotor, Philadelphia, PA; Craig Miller, public relations, USA Basketball, Colorado Springs, CO; Michael Ranft, CA Hot Springs, AK; Andrew Clary, ATC, Head Athletic Trainer, University of Miami (FL); Hannah Bradford, American Association of Acupuncture and Oriental Medicine; Lori Warner, Public Relations Coordinator, National Strength and Conditioning Association, Lincoln, NE; Michael Billauer, D.C., Billauer Chiropractic Offices, Marina Del Rey, CA, and Team Physician, Men's U.S. Volleyball Olympic Team (1988); Marilee Matheny, M.S., Director of Fitness Program, Shiley Sports and Health Center of Scripps Clinic, San Diego, CA; Michael Colgan, Ph.D., Director, Colgan Institute, Encinitas, CA; Larry Shane, Athletic Department, Villanova University; Michele Sharp, Women's Basketball Coach, Northwich University, Northfield, VT; Trudy Tappan, Ed.D., Health Science Specialist, Richmond, VA; Dick Borkowski, Ed.D., AD the Episcopal Academy (Merion, PA) and Sports Safety and Law Specialist; Ron Barr, host, and Larry Maxwell, producer, "Sports Byline" National Radio Talk Show; Don Hunt, media specialist and free-lance sportswriter, Philadelphia, PA; Glenn Tuckett, Director of Athletics, Brigham Young University; Bonnie Bekkan, editor (Social Studies School Service) and free-lance writer; Larry Matthews, Ed.D., Associate Athletic Director, Yale University; Fred Hickman, CNN Sports; Bill Brosseau, coach, Tolt H.S., Carnation, OR; Wendy Heffernan, sales associate, Foot Locker; Maureen Lewis, Assistant Director of Public Relations, Washington Bullets, NBA; Charles Watkins, Management Strategies Unlimited, Washington, DC; NY Chiropractic College;

Paul Smith, sportswriter, *News Dispatch,* Michigan City, IN; Bucky Grace, Kirkwood Fitness Center, Edgemont, PA; Howie Long, Los Angeles Raiders, NFL; Gabe Merkin, M.D., The Sports Medicine Institute, Silver Spring, MD, and Associate Clinical Professor, Georgetown University; Ted Aceto, Villanova University; Joe Crawford, NBA Official; Monique Berlioux, Comite International Olympique; Berny Wagner, Executive Director, Track and Field Association, U.S.A.; Roy Rylander, Ph.D., University of Delaware; Major Ranko Sopko, U.S.A., Administrative Officer, Office of the Director of Intercollegiate Athletics, U.S. Military Academy; James McHugh, Director of Procurement, U.S. Olympic Committee; Anne Moss, *Backstretch* magazine; Ed Miersch, Sports Physical Therapists, Bryn Mawr, PA; Gerry Kaplan, AD, basketball coach, O'Neil High School, New York; Ed Kershner, Tredyfrin-Easttown School District, PA; Stephanie Gaitley, women's basketball coach, St. Joseph's (PA) University; Ted Town, Assistant Executive Director, National Collegiate Athletic Association; Ted Quendenfeld, Administrative Director, Temple University Center for Sports Medicine and Science; Harold J. Vanderzwagg, Department Head, Social Studies, The University of Massachusetts; Marty Walsh, Football, Baseball Official, Newark, DE; Michael Sachs, University of Maryland Medical School; Harry Wendelstadt, Major League Baseball umpire and baseball school director.

A special thank you is made to Kelly Green, to Mary and Rick Heitzmann, and to Villanova University.

A special dedication is made to the basketball, baseball, and football players I've coached, and to the sports people with whom I've worked.

FOREWORD

The exciting and glamorous life we envision professional athletes leading is the pinnacle of sports achievement. But these high-profile, much sought after jobs are not the only positions available in this ever-expanding career field. Sports and athletics require much more than the fan entertainment the athletes offer to make sports successful at all levels of competition.

The job opportunities that service sports and athletics in general outnumber those of athletes many times over. From physical education in the school setting to coaching pee-wees or managing the big leagues, from sports medicine to sports officiating, the peripheral jobs supporting the players are the real substance of sports and athletics the world over.

Athletes who can no longer compete at the professional level, or instructors who wish to teach others how to play, or those enthusiasts who just want to be near the action, all gravitate toward jobs in this field for the same basic reason: their love of sport. *Opportunities in Sports and Athletics Careers* gives you an overview of the opportunities in the sporting and athletic fields. Dr. William Ray Heitzmann provides the information you need to find out where to attend the right schools for your goals, how to meet people in the field you wish to enter, and most importantly what kinds of jobs are available for those wishing to enjoy a career in sports.

As you enter the field, remember that those people on the sidelines and in the offices, or working the cameras or writing the reviews, maintain the popularity of sports in the United States today as much as any athlete ever has. There are only a small percentage of people entering the sporting field as athletes, and deservedly they receive the accolades that go with the hard work they have put into producing the excellence that fans want and expect from them. The greater number of jobs in sports and athletics, however, have to do with what happens off the field of play, and here is where the true love of "the game" can be found.

The Editors
VGM Career Books

INTRODUCTION

He has participated in the Mirage Bowl, Emerald Isle Classic, the Peach Bowl, and football games coast to coast. He is most proud of the game ball he received in a big win over Memphis State.

Who is this? Dick Hall, head equipment manager, USMA at West Point!

Dick typifies those who love and wish to stay close to sports during their lives. He graduated from high school and found himself in the Army shortly thereafter. Following service in Vietnam he obtained a position in the athletic equipment room at West Point. Soon he moved up to assistant manager and finally to head equipment manager. One of his many successes came during the Memphis State–Army football game. An unexpected drop in temperature prior to the game combined with snow made the artificial turf a skating pond! The team's regular shoes did not help. He took a chance and tried molded sole shoes normally used on grass for a few players—they worked great. He quickly outfitted the team—the result—Army 49 Memphis State 7! "As an equipment manager you never know what kind of weather problems, what kind of equipment failure, or what kind of transportation problems you may encounter. You have to roll with the problems just like player or coach," believes Hall. "It's not boring and really makes for an enjoyable life when you love sports and athletic competition."

There exists an explosion of sports in North America and around the world. The expansion of minor sports, women's sports, athletic tournaments, all-star games, club sports, and community teams continues unabated. This dramatic growth has resulted in a comparable major development of related careers in sports and athletics. Consequently, regardless of your personal interests and skills—computers, landscaping, biology, sales, writing—there exist numerous options. *There is a job in sports for you.*

Careers in this area divide into two general categories: science and humanities. The latter includes specialties such as writing, agents, television and radio, management, and related fields. The former involves athletic training, strength and conditioning specialist, statistician, massage therapist, acupuncturist, orthopedic surgeon, and related areas.

Read the entire book. It will give you a total view of the range of athletic professions. Furthermore, sports careers are greatly interrelated; for example, behind every successful coach there exists a horde of support personnel—an agent negotiates the contract, scouts and statisticians provide valuable data on the opponents, public relations specialists promote the team, a strength and flexibility coach trains the players, an athletic trainer conditions and assists with injuries, sports marketing people coordinate advertising and manage ticket sales, and so on.

In the author's experience with athletics and during the preparation of this book and other publications on sports, three factors become paramount. First, there exists great dedication marked by long hours of work. Typical is Jim Rohr, assistant general manager of the Toledo Mud Hens, A Detroit Tigers baseball minor league affiliate. On game day he gets to the office early and doesn't leave until an hour or so after the night game ends!

Shelly Pennefather, following an outstanding college basketball career resulting in selection as women's player of the year, wanted to continue playing the game. She played professionally in Japan!

While attending the University of Maryland, Alan Alper assisted Bethesda–Chevy Chase High School as athletic trainer; he received $450.00 however, averaging 50 hours per week for the school year, for a total of $0.75 per hour!

Second, there exists great job satisfaction. June Hannah, wife of University of Delaware's very successful baseball coach, nicely summarizes the situation: "I don't mind the number of hours Bob spends with baseball. I'm just happy he is so happy with his career when so many others dislike their jobs."

Third, there has been a dramatic growth in the professionalism of sports, fitness, and athletics-related careers. For example, the National Operating Committee on the Standards for Athletic Equipment (NOCSAE, Kansas City, MO) has expanded its visibility and efforts to evaluate equipment and assist in prevention of athletic injuries.

Often associated with this growing professionalism are training and education programs leading to certification. Those interested in sports nutrition and its potential to maximize athletic performance might be interested in the new National Certification Program in Nutrition conducted by Dr. Michael Colgan (Colgan Institute, Encinitas, CA). Aerobic instructors can improve their knowledge and skills through the programs of AAAI–ISMA (American Aerobic Association International–International Sports Medicine Association, Richboro, PA). Courses in Primary Aerobic Instructor Certification, Master/Step Aerobic Instructor Certification, Aerobic Program Director Certification, and Personal Fitness Trainer offer the opportunity to develop professionally, assisting not only the participant but also eventually clients and students.

Professional developments have improved the procedures in the area of the strength and conditioning specialist. As with other organizations, the National Strength and Conditioning Association (NSCA, Lincoln, NE) offers courses, videotapes, publications, and certification.

Throughout the realm of sports and athletics, professional organizations exist to provide preservice training and education (often through schools) and continuing education; this book will detail them.

This book, although primarily written for high school students, will find a home among college students, those contemplating mid-life job changes, and even early retirees! The book emphasizes the major opportunities and provides information on the career and avenues to enter it. A special effort has been made to suggest methods in which you can prepare yourself for positions described.

Outsiders often see only the glamour of athletic and sports careers—observing the limelight, big bucks, glory, and recognition. Contemplate the words of Joe Crawford, successful veteran of fifteen years of the wars of professional basketball: "When you first get into this racket it is exciting and glamorous, but that fades after a couple of years it becomes just a job." Crawford, who has officiated the NBA finals for the last six years, states "many times it's 22 hours of boredom for 2 hours of excitement, it's not all glory!" In addition, for every sports figure who is a household word there are 100 laboring in the shadows—and these unknowns (or locally knowns) love what they are doing.

It's the author's hope that this book will contribute to the reader's understanding of athletic careers and will aid him or her in entering the wonderful world of sports.

CONTENTS

About the Author . . . . **iii**

Acknowledgments . . . . **v**

Foreword . . . . **ix**

Introduction . . . . **xi**

1. **Professional Athletes** **1**

Health and fitness. Career preparation. Training and conditioning. Women: myths destroyed. Mental preparation:
positive attitude, confidence, mental edge, psyche, intelligence. Mental toughness. Nutrition. Getting started.
What if? Final suggestions.

2. **Coaching Careers** **17**

The school coach. Professional coaching. Volunteer
coach. Preparing to coach.

3. **Sports Administration** **33**

School athletic director. Professional and other positions.
Education.

4. **Sports Officiating** 41
    Officiating guidelines. Getting started. Officiating
    schools. Preparing for your future.

5. **Sports Journalism** 53
    Newspaper sportswriting. Preparing for your career.
    Sportscaster. How to begin.

6. **Physical Education** 63
    Duties and activities. A typical day. Education. Getting
    started.

7. **Sports Medicine** 73
    New orientation. Athletic trainers. Education. Sports phy-
    sician. Orthopedist. Osteopath. Chiropractor. Summary—
    sports physicians. Physical therapy. Paraprofessionals.
    Other sports medicine opportunities. Sports medicine clin-
    ics and centers. Getting started.

8. **Public Relations** 93
    Professional teams. College positions. Getting started.

9. **Additional Sports Careers** 101
    Sports equipment sales and development. Sports psycholo-
    gist. Sports photographer—still and motion. Agents and
    sports representatives. Health and fitness specialists.
    Sports facility maintenance personnel. Complementary
    health therapies. Stadium and arena concessionaires.
    Sports instructor. Sports entrepreneur. Statisticians.
    Sports cartoonist. Scout. Sports academicians. Equip-
    ment manager. Future careers.

Appendix A: Sports and Athletics Organizations 125

Appendix B: Sports and Athletics Organizations for Those with Special Needs 133

Appendix C: Sports Museums and Halls of Fame 135

Appendix D: Magazines and Newspapers 141

CHAPTER 1

PROFESSIONAL ATHLETES

There probably exists no man or woman who at some point has not entertained the fantasy of becoming a professional athlete. The salaries, the public adulation, and the opportunity to play are far too much for all of us to resist. Fortunately, a wide variety of sports exists from which to choose to prepare yourself. Regardless of the sport(s) chosen, it will be a long, rigorous battle that will test the physical skills and character of aspiring athletes. Only those with great desire and intensity, meshed with the appropriate physical and mental skills, will enter the select circle. The road remains difficult, but the rewards make the effort worthwhile.

The limelight in the United States and Canada shines brightly on successful athletes. This hero worship, sometimes misplaced, shows no sign of discontinuing. A recent poll conducted by *Research and Forecasts* found that an amazing 96.3 percent of the American public are involved in sports. Furthermore, a full 44 percent of Americans participated in some kind of athletic activities on a daily basis.

HEALTH AND FITNESS

Athletics have been justified in schools and society for several reasons. Among other things, athletics provide for the physical develop-

1

ment of young people. While some of our citizens shorten their life expectancy because of eating habits and sedentary behavior, there exists a growing movement toward improved nutrition and physical fitness. In accord with this recent direction by the general public, schools have begun to transmit to students the knowledge, attitudes, and skills necessary for well-being and happiness.

However, physical education specialists more than any teachable group have neglected to secure converts to the objectives of their program. Perhaps their traditional involvement in interscholastic athletics (which likewise needs support) has drained their energies, depriving them of communicating the values of fitness and sports.

Despite some wonderfully successful activities—such as the "People to People Sports" programs, The Special Olympics, and the programs of the President's Council on Physical Fitness and Sports—there are far too many young people who have not profited from good health and fitness. One study conducted in ten states found that 39 percent of the boys and 33 percent of the girls aged 11–18 were overweight. Further studies show that an overweight 12-year-old has only a 20 percent chance of being a normal weighted adult. By age 18 that chance drops to 5 percent!

Some serious studies have been undertaken in the area of youth fitness. The 1965 report showed dramatic gains for students over the 1958 results. However, the 1975 report concluded that the physical fitness of the public school children in the continental United States showed little or no improvement in ten years. Recent reports have shown students making a slow, but positive improvement in fitness. Clearly, schools, communities, social and professional organizations, and, most importantly, families, need to give more attention to youth fitness.

A wave of interest in fitness has spread in America's adult community. Taking the form of jogging-running and health spa workouts (presently over 3,000 health clubs exist), the good health orientation has trickled down to young people. Health America, a group composed of athletes, physicians, and politicians, maintains that the health of Americans would benefit more from increasing the number of swimming pools and running/jogging paths than from adding new hospital beds. The group hopes to work actively to reduce sedentary living, excessive eating, alcoholism, hypertension, and smoking.

To some extent this reinterest in fitness has come from what has come to be known as the "new" fitness. This orientation emphasizes a mental, spiritual, and physical approach characterized by noncompetitiveness and fun. Similarly, many young people want to preserve their bodies and remain youthful through exercise and good nutrition. Nutrition gained an important boost from Senator George McGovern's Select Committee on Nutrition and Human Needs, which criticized many of America's junk food eating habits.

Sports involvement makes a major contribution to the physical well-being of the participants.

Character

Sports has the potential to build character among the players. That is, the self-discipline, teamwork, sacrifice, and fair play that are so much a part of sports, teach strong character skills. Generally, with a growing number of noticeable exceptions, sports has done this. Furthermore, it provides preparation for life or life adjustment.

A game, a season for the players and team, closely mirrors life. There are high periods when everything goes exactly right for the players and the team, such as a last-second victory or clinching a playoff spot. There are also stretches of terrible lows when nothing goes right, like fouling out of a game or committing a game-losing mistake. Life is much the same. We all may experience great happiness—a salary bonus, the birth of a child, a community award, or some recognition. Conversely, there are unhappy events—the death of a loved one, the loss of a job, or even the receipt of a traffic ticket. Sports participation permits the athlete to experience adversity. The highs and lows involved in sports offer an excellent preparation for life's stresses and struggles.

CAREER PREPARATION

Professional athletes know it but often those aspiring to become pros do not: that is, almost life-long preparation is necessary prior to playing professional sports. Some specifics follow. In a recent issue of *The American Journal of Sports Medicine,* Dr. Jack Hughston shared with his readers the Six D's of Success of Coach "Shug" Jordan of Auburn University:

Discipline—Self-discipline as well as the ability to take discipline from others is the first step to success.

Desire to excel—This motivation exists as a must, not only for ball players but everyone. In addition, this means getting the most out of every practice.

Determination—The desire to keep on trying regardless of setbacks such as a bad play or an injury.

Dedication—A commitment to your goal that carries with it the sacrifice that is necessary for success.

Dependability—Reliability and consistency is the mark of the "pro." Coaches must know that a player can be counted upon to contribute in many situations. It also means the small things, such as being on time for the bus leaving for the game and manifesting responsibility when given a job to perform.

Darn it, anyway—When everything seems against you and nothing seems to work, do something—but don't give up. Sometimes an action disrupts the harmony or flow of your opponent, permitting you to reverse the situation.

The above offer some suggestions; following are some guidelines on Training and Conditioning, Mental Preparation, and Nutrition.

TRAINING AND CONDITIONING

Visual Enhancement, Eat to Win, Motion Analysis, Plyometric Training, Guided Fantasy (Mental Rehearsal)

The science of sports has resulted in a number of proven strategies to enhance athletic performance. In addition to the numerous hours on the playing field, prospective professional athletes must avail themselves of the latest developments to ensure every chance of success.

Coupled with born ability must be a burning desire, dedication, enthusiasm, and belief in one's self. For without this, all the work in the world will not result in success.

The growing sophistication of sport science, with new inventions and procedures occurring almost daily, requires the athlete to work closely with a team or individual coach. With the odds heavily stacked against the prospect of success, the enjoyment of the means (training and conditioning) and of intermediate successes (all-star games) must be relished during the improbable but possible journey to employment in professional sports.

WOMEN: MYTHS DESTROYED

The national and international success of women's athletics has captured the attention of all sports fans. Just a decade and a half ago female athletes were thought too frail to participate in sports to the extent they do today. Athletics were believed too demanding and too intense except for men.

Fortunately, the myth that women cannot engage in conditioning and training activities has quickly disappeared. Professor George Colfer, Texas A&M University, has reviewed the research on women and physical activity and developed the following conclusions:

1. One can be athletically skilled and trained rigorously without any loss of femininity.
2. Women are perfectly capable of performing strenuous activity without any physiological impairment.
3. Active women possess a better state of health than those who are inactive.
4. Women are capable of high-level motor tasks as well as those involving endurance capacities.
5. Strength can be developed or improved in women at a higher ratio than that of men.

Colfer concluded that the training needs of women are basically the same as men and there is no reason to invent unique training techniques for women.

Although further research is needed, some studies show that women receive proportionately more injuries than men. Dr. Christine Haycock, a physician and sports medicine specialist, feels this results from improper equipment, particularly in the area of footwear and bras, and the lack of proper training facilities. Joan Gilette, trainer, University of Oklahoma, following an extensive survey of the common injuries incurred by women, concluded that improper training methods, including a deficit of precollege conditioning and lack of modern training methods, are major factors in women's injuries. She specifically suggests screening programs to identify poorly conditioned athletes; preseason, in-season, and postseason training using weights; and earlier participation.

Opportunities for women in athletics have expanded greatly. At the high school level almost two million women participate in interscholastic sports. Most major colleges offer athletic scholarships for women. And women's professional basketball has gotten off to a slow but healthy start on the international level.

While there exists some debate over certain aspects of conditioning and training, most coaches and trainers agree on the main emphasis (see

Sports Medicine chapter for guidelines)—weight training, endurance, agility, stretching and running for speed, and cardiovascular strength. Prior to beginning any program, an athlete should consult with a knowledgeable person as to procedures so as to maximize her or his efforts and to avoid injury. Weight conditioning brings gains of strength and power, reduces injuries, and builds confidence. While some opportunities exist at school gyms or health clubs, owning your personal set of free weights will offer increased opportunities to work out. You may wish to consider purchasing secondhand equipment and setting up your own gym; schools, the YMCAs and other groups sell used equipment through classified ads when purchasing new equipment. Some companies offer relatively inexpensive and useful home use equipment that can aid in physical development.

Several studies have examined various sports in terms of their contribution to fitness (and, of course, the sports' demands upon the player). Based upon a 1–10 system, a list of sports ratings as to muscle, lung, and heart requirements follows:

Auto racing	3	Ice hockey	7
Baseball	3	Judo	7
Basketball	8	Lacrosse	6
Bicycling	4	Marathon	9
Boxing	9	Paddleball	4
Cross-country	6	Relay racing	6
Decathlon	10	Rodeo	3
Field hockey	6	Scuba diving	3
Football	7	Swimming	6
Handball	8	Weight lifting	4

The President's Council on Physical Fitness has developed the following chart (scale 0–21):

	Jogging	Swimming	Basketball	Tennis	Calisthenics	Golf	Bowling
Cardio-respiratory (endurance; stamina)	21	21	19	16	10	8	5
Muscular endurance	20	20	17	16	13	8	5
Muscular strength	17	14	15	14	16	9	5
Flexibility	9	15	13	14	19	8	7
Balance	17	12	16	16	15	8	6
Weight control	21	15	19	16	16	6	5
Muscle definition	14	14	14	13	18	6	5
Digestion	13	13	10	12	11	7	7
Sleep	16	16	12	11	12	6	6

The chart above provides information on how demanding the sport(s) of your choice will be—your training should follow accordingly. Be sure to include a program of flexibility. Consequently, stretching has become part of every coach's and athlete's program to avoid injury.

"Paying the price," long a slogan in sports, has no greater application than in the area of physical conditioning and training. For some, the price is too great unless looked upon in a positive fashion. That is, the process can be as enjoyable as the product—athletic success.

MENTAL PREPARATION: POSITIVE ATTITUDE, CONFIDENCE, MENTAL EDGE, PSYCHE, INTELLIGENCE

Few make it to any type of athletic success today unless they have the "sound mind" to accompany the "sound body." Among basketball coaches in Illinois there exists a generally agreed-upon belief that "it takes heady guards to go downstate." That means unless a team has smart guards who can analyze changing defenses, break presses, and control the tempo of the game, it has little chance of making it to the state tournament. Today's sports are a sophisticated business—the person who doesn't make it in the classroom will have serious difficulties on the court or field. Perhaps this is why research tells us that athletes as a group outperform their fellow students in academics.

In the past, some athletes have obtained the stigma of dullards (and perhaps a few deserved it). Today's coaches avoid the player who has a poor academic record because that student will have eligibility problems as well as difficulty understanding offensive and defensive systems. Today's high school, college, and pro teams not only have many plays but they often are quite complicated. As sports become more complex, the mental power of athletes will need to keep pace accordingly. Remember, doing well in the classroom will contribute to your athletic performance.

MENTAL TOUGHNESS

On a regular, daily basis a positive mental attitude remains a must for success in athletics. Players must rise above the adversity of a particular situation to become successful. Far too often, the inexperienced player will compound a mistake by making another mistake.

Steve Carlton practiced "positive pitching" to achieve success for the Philadelphia Phillies. Coaches use "psychocybernetics" or similar techniques to develop their players' confidence. Coach Patricia Hannisch, Kean College, New Jersey, feels that confidence comes when a player is sure of her or his ability, as a result of having successful experiences. Talking of her own confidence game, golfer Janie Blalock says that for a while she could compensate for her poor playing by thinking more and by playing the percentages. She never expected to hit bad shots but subconsciously made allowances. Most good athletes have this ability to adapt their games on off-days. It's a resilience—something that makes you hang in there no matter how badly you're playing. If players don't have confidence in themselves, who else will? A little cockiness will not hurt.

The true test of a winning attitude comes late in a game when a big play is needed. Winners make those plays—they want the ball—they know they can do it. Losers think of excuses, prefer not to be in the game, wish the ball would not come to them. Winning and losing become habits. Make your habit winning.

NUTRITION

The movement toward good nutrition and supplementation with vitamins, herbs, and minerals is obvious. Prospective athletes must remain particularly cautious of their food consumption. This can be a difficult task. The Select Committee on Nutrition and Human Needs, U.S. Senate, recently released a report very critical of American eating habits. Unfortunately, young people are the worst victims of this diet.

Eat a "power breakfast"—complex carbohydrates, protein, fruit, and caffeine-free fluids, every day. This will feed your brain and body, assisting you in school work and on the playing field. Unfortunately, a recent noticeable negative trend toward skipping breakfast (or eating heavily sugared cereals) has developed, seriously damaging the performance of potential athletes. Professional athletes should serve as models, even missionaries, carrying the wellness and fitness message to peers.

Several studies of school lunches found many of them lacking in some important areas and overly abundant in refined carbohydrates and fats. If your school lacks nutritional lunches, take your own. Additionally, avoid the junk food that provides little help to your physical development. Likewise, follow the suggestions of many champions who carefully watch what they eat, and don't drink alcohol or smoke.

Combining rest, relaxation, sleep, and physical training with a proper nutritional plan, and a sense of self confidence, will aid you in the direction of athletic success. In fact, it's a must.

GETTING STARTED

The variety of sports results in varying methods of entering the ranks of professional athletics. Most prospective athletes begin sports at the lower levels—Little League, Pop Warner programs, CYO, YMCA, and others, and then participate at the school they attend. Successful playing may result in a college scholarship or a contract offer. Even if this does not occur, a student can continue to play at college and/or on a local team and work to improve. Following signing a professional contract, some players enter the minor leagues; others get a direct shot at the pros. Those not making the team will often play with a semipro team and try again next season.

Life in the minor leagues tests the players' character and desire. In Dave Klein's *On The Way Up* (Messner), George Brett, the third baseman of the Kansas City Royals baseball team, tells how he felt when he was assigned to Billings, Montana, in the Pioneer League. Since baseball was still his most important priority, he was determined not to spend many more years in the minors. To use up his free time, he got involved in photography, as did some other players on the team. Photography provided a different outlet. After reaching the majors and performing exceptionally well (he's played in the All-Star game several times), he recalled another thing he learned in the minors: to keep setting higher goals. Once a player is too satisfied, he or she is ready for a trip down to the minor leagues.

Other sports provide different means to make it as a pro. The following are examples. *Golf* uses an apprenticeship program to train club professionals and approved tournament players; there also are PGA tour qualifying schools. For additional information, contact:

The Professional Golfers' Association of America
804 Federal Highway
Box 12458
Lake Park, FL 33403

Similarly, a career in *ski instruction* requires apprenticeship training. Specifics can be obtained from:

Professional Ski Instructors of America
1726 Champa, Room 300
Denver, CO 80202

Tennis teaching closely follows the form of the above professions. The three schools listed below certify potential tennis instructors. Also listed is the professional association:

Vic Braden's U.S. Tennis Academy
P.O. Box 438
Trabuco Canyon, CA 92678

Dennis Van Der Meer's Tennis University
2150 Franklin St., Suite 580
Oakland, CA 94612

USPTA School
Colony Beach and Tennis Resort
1620 Gulf of Mexico Drive
Longboat Key
Sarasota, FL 33548

United States Tennis Association
51 East 42nd Street
New York, NY 10017

Don't overlook the *rodeo life*—in recent years salaries have expanded greatly; it's not unusual for the top riders to be in the $100,000-a-year range! Additional careers exist as timers, clowns, and announcers. Contact:

Professional Rodeo Cowboys Association
2929 West 19th Avenue
Denver, CO 80204

Numerous opportunities exist in *horse racing,* the "sport of kings," and related professions. These careers take a very special expertise and experience remains a must. To become a thoroughbred horse trainer, write to the following for advice:

United Thoroughbred Trainers Association
19363 James Couzens Highway
Detroit, MI 48235

Information related to the many trotting jobs may be obtained from:

The United States Trotting Association
750 Michigan Avenue
Columbus, OH 43215

Boxers should investigate the Golden Gloves as a vehicle to make it into the profession. Write:

Golden Gloves Association of America
8801 Princess Jeanned, N.E.
Albuquerque, NM 87112

Professional wrestling, the fastest growing sport of the past decade, can offer a challenging career. Several schools exist around the country to train these skilled performers and those in related jobs like ring announcer, manager, referee, and so on. Some of these schools include:

Chris Adams
Cola Productions
P.O. Box 190340
Dallas, TX 75219

Heart of American Sports
910 Penn, Suite 305
Kansas City, MO 64105

Johnny Valiant's Pro Wrestling Camp
7959 Golf Road
Suite 99
Morton Grove, IL 60053

Killer Kowalski's Wrestling School
P.O. Box 67
Reading, MA 08167

Monster Factory
P.O. Box 345
Westville, NJ 08093

The Heide Lee Morgan School of Professional Wrestling
274 Route 40
Newfield, NJ 98344
(women only)

Ringmaster's Wrestling School
P.O. Box 57068
Philadelphia, PA 19111

Rodz-Gleason's Wrestling School
21 Front Street
Brooklyn, NY 11201
(also has a special program to train teen-agers ages 16, 17, and 18
in professional wrestling)

Slammers Wrestling Gym
P.O. Box 1602
Studio City, CA 91614

The Wild Samons Pro Wrestling Training Center
719 Jordon Long Parkway
Whitehall, PA 18052

Don't overlook professional *bowling;* while most bowlers participate as a hobby (with total dedication), some sporting goods companies offer full-time positions. For information, women may contact:

Women's Professional Bowlers Association
   205 W. Wacker Drive, Suite 300
   Chicago, Illinois 60606

Addresses for other professional associations may be found in Appendixes A and B in the back of this book.

WHAT IF?

What if you don't make it? The odds are against you—about 1,000 to 1! Only 1,200 make it in the NFL; 250 in the NBA; 360 in the NHL; 100 in boxing, etc. Don't be fooled by the appearance of new leagues and the expansion into new teams in the United States, Canada and abroad.

In considering your future as a professional athlete, work hard to make it, but plan for your future as if you don't have a chance. Remember it is better to have tried and not succeeded than never to have tried at all.

What if you do make it? In addition to a continuing commitment to improving yourself and giving time and service back to the society that supports you, prepare for the day your career ends. Recently, Gayle Sayers was asked to explain why he's been so successful after his football career. He answered that just as he had trained hard for football, he had prepared well for his life after it. Stories of players who foolishly spent their salaries and ended their careers penniless are numerous. For most players, the transition from the glory and the limelight back to "ordinary" life is difficult enough; it should not be compounded by financial problems or anxiety related to job hunting. With proper preparation, most athletes can use sports as a springboard to a fine second career. Many opportunities exist in sports; in addition, business and industry often seek out athletes for employment.

FINAL SUGGESTIONS

In preparing for professional sports, follow these guidelines:

1. Read all you can about your sport—particularly the "How to" books and magazines.
2. Organize a plan for yourself for physical development. Enter events such as "Pitch, Hit, and Run" contests, qualify for a "Presidential Sports Award" and/or "President's Physical Fitness Award" and similar programs.
3. Practice, practice, practice, on your own, with others, and on organized teams. Join organizations (YMCA, YWCA, CYO, JCC, Boy Scouts, Girl Scouts, Little League, and others). Try out for the local teams, the Special Olympics, the Olympics.
4. Build a nutritional sense. Avoid those foods that may hurt your development and choose foods and supplements that will contribute to your growth.
5. Join the professional organization related to your sporting interest, if one exists.
6. Demonstrate a positive mental attitude. Build self-confidence. *Become a winner not only in sports but also in life.*

CHAPTER 2

COACHING CAREERS

"A window of opportunity exists to help young people, permitting a coach to help a kid not only on the playing field but in life. I know this sounds trite but it's true."

Coach Bill Brosseau,
Tolt High School Carnation, Washington

Following graduation from Salem College in West Virginia, Brosseau began coaching (football, track, lacrosse) and teaching (physical education) in New York State. A part-time job in a health club combined with a long-time interest in weight training and physical conditioning eventually led to a full-time position in sales and management in the fitness equipment field. However, "I wanted to return to a school situation; one wonderful aspect of physical education teaching is these kids come to class excited and ready." At Tolt Brosseau teaches two electives dealing with "strength conditioning and fitness development. I enjoy it greatly." In addition, he works on curriculum development, integrating physical education with academic subjects.

Brosseau serves as an assistant football coach at his school and in the community as head coach for lacrosse. "My background in strength training has greatly helped me to assist my players and in turn improve their performance and that of our teams." Coach William Brosseau reflects well upon his school and the coaching profession.

Unfortunately there exists a major crisis in America's coaching profession. Basically it has attracted insufficient people. Consequently some schools and other teams at all levels have settled for coaches with limited experience and on occasion little interest! This has resulted in a number of tragic situations. Novice coaches have obtained head varsity positions without sufficient knowledge of their sport (normally acquired in the ranks of assistant coaching, through reading, observation of many contests, and participation at summer camps and clinics). Often many rookies compound this defeat with a lack of knowledge of children. The result: many quit or are asked to leave after a couple of years and because of this early negative experience are lost to the profession. Of course some continue in coaching improving their skills and record; some move to lower levels (middle school, junior high) or become assistant coaches.

Despite attempts to reduce the emphasis upon winning, the demands upon coaches remain heavy. Players want to improve, parents want their children to learn skills and be competitive, administrators want to see practices, travel, games, events conducted in an efficient, well-organized fashion. Even with these requirements most coaches love their job.

The opportunity of having a positive effect on young people is probably more available in coaching than in any other sports career. Thousands of coaches at all levels labor daily to develop their players to win games or events. The profession can be very rewarding, challenging, and self-fulfilling; but many days are hectic, tiring, and, unfortunately, thankless. Recently some coaches have openly expressed their disappointment in the lack of dedication of some athletes, that is, players who have sidetracked themselves—watching television, playing video games or "hanging out"—instead of committing themselves to self-improvement. Fortunately, the majority of athletes are more dedicated.

No one should coach unless he or she is familiar with and can implement The Bill of Rights for Young Athletes. It serves as an excellent guideline for youth program coaches. Some "rights" apply to coaches of high school and older players.

The Bill of Rights for Young Athletes

1. Right of the opportunity to participate in sports regardless of ability level.
2. Right to participate at a level that is commensurate with each child's development level.
3. Right to have qualified adult leadership.
4. Right to participate in safe, healthy environments.
5. Right of each child to share in the leadership and decision making of their sport participation.
6. Right to play as a child and not as an adult.
7. Right to proper preparation for participation in the sport.
8. Right to equal opportunity to strive for success.
9. Right to be treated with dignity by all involved.
10. Right to have fun through sport.

THE SCHOOL COACH

Assistant Coach

Opportunities, opportunities, opportunities.

The expansion of minor sports, such as hockey, soccer, lacrosse, field hockey, power lifting, and wrestling, and the explosion of women's sports have created a serious need for new persons to enter the profession. At some schools programs such as freshman track and women's junior varsity volleyball have been discontinued for lack of coaching staff.

Almost all public and private schools have interscholastic athletic teams which compete against those of other schools. In some states, coaches have taken certain certification courses; in others only certified educators may coach. However, it is possible in most public and private schools to obtain employment in a part-time situation.

Is it necessary to be a physical education teacher to serve as a coach? No, most schools would not have enough coaches if this were a policy.

In fact, many classroom teachers of various subjects enjoy the variety that their involvement with school sports permits. Many teachers believe that their involvement in after-school activities with students helps them to be more successful in the classroom.

How can you get started in coaching? As with other careers, you should begin as early as possible. (Some specific suggestions can be found later in this chapter—see Preparing to Coach.)

When you apply for a teaching position, indicate your willingness to serve as a sports coach. In many schools this will aid you to obtain employment. During your employment interview, express your interest. If no opening exists, volunteer to help in scouting or other ways. Most coaches will be only too willing to have an additional assistant if the person has some knowledge, is conscientious, and can provide a service. Very few head coaches have the time necessary to extensively train or monitor an assistant's progress, so the volunteer must be a positive asset rather than a liability.

Most coaches begin their careers serving as assistant coaches, working with teams at the lower levels such as eighth grade, freshman, or junior varsity. This situation (in which the person functions as a head coach) presents a wonderful opportunity. You can gain experience working with young people while experimenting with your own offensive and defensive systems and, most importantly, learning how to teach the sport. Most successful coaches are not only knowledgeable about their sport but have the ability to transfer that knowledge to the players. Most often this ability can be developed in coaching younger players in games played after school or Saturday mornings. Consequently, an assignment to a team at this level should be looked upon as an opportunity for self-development; it deserves a serious commitment that will be mutually advantageous to you and to the players. Coach Don Casey, Boston Celtics professional basketball team assistant coach, believes that every coach should serve an apprenticeship working with teams at the high school level to gain experience playing against a variety of offenses and defenses in various situations. Casey served as basketball coach at Bishop Eustace High School (Pennsauken, NJ), assistant and then head coach at Temple University in Philadelphia, and assistant coach with the Chicago Bulls and LA Clippers prior to joining the NBA's Celtics.

Head Coach

No one aspires to the position of assistant coach; frequently, it is a demanding position with little recognition. However, your players will realize your ability as will the opposing coaches and your own head coach. Eventually this may result in your promotion to the position of head coach at your school or another.

Head coaches of varsity teams perform many of the same tasks as their counterparts at lower levels except that they have greater visibility, larger audiences (and frequently critics), more responsibility, and, consequently, more accountability. That is, the job is more exciting, rewarding, and glamorous, but the head coach also has greater pressure for success.

Coaching Duties

In the head coaching position there exist tremendous time pressures—more jobs need to be completed than the outsider may realize.

In addition to preparing for normal teaching duties, head coaches spend numerous hours in preparation for their coaching. Here is a partial list of typical activities:

Discussing scheduling with athletic director, school administrators, and opposing coaches;
Arranging for preseason scrimmage games;
Recruiting team managers and statisticians;
Meeting regularly with assistant coaches;
Making a schedule for scouting opponents;
Announcing tryouts;
Writing press releases for newspapers;
Planning for use of athletic facilities;

Choosing the team and selecting the starting team;
Studying scouting and analyzing your opponents;
Creating a game plan;
Planning and organizing daily practices;
Clipping newspaper stories on your opponents and your team;
Inviting the players' parents to the games;
Asking knowledgeable persons to scout your team for weaknesses;
Arranging for filming (or videotaping) of your team;
Encouraging players to attend summer sports camp and participate in
    summer sports;
Attending educational conferences for athletic coaches;
Discussing the program (and problems) with the school principal, the
    athletic director, and other administrators;
Writing thank-you letters to appropriate individuals;
Taking inventory and ordering new equipment;
Studying proposed rule changes;
Evaluating the success of the program, including wins and losses.

If the above list looks like difficult work, you are correct; coaching is not easy. At the school level, few enter for financial reasons. Perhaps the numerous required duties lead many coaches to early retirement. It should be remembered that coaches have regular teaching duties to properly execute (such as class preparation, test correction, and course planning) as their primary obligation.

Because of those who leave coaching and the expansion of sports, many opportunities exist for coaching employment. Salaries vary with the emphasis the community places upon the sport. For example, a school district which regards football as very important may pay a coach as much as $5,000 a season; generally, coaches of major sports—football, basketball, baseball—receive salaries of around $3,000, while coaches of minor sports (tennis, wrestling, swimming) receive around $1,500, unless there is strong local interest. Naturally this is in addition to a teaching salary.

An increasing number of coaches have primary employment outside the school. Their job permits the flexibility to attend practices and games; coaches in these situations need to make an extra effort to become involved in school activities (attend school fair, school play, etc.) to develop relationships with administrators, faculty, and students. At the school level, coaching, which is really an avocation, offers the opportunity to work very closely with a group of young people and have a very large impact upon their development. Many of the friendships made will be carried throughout the coach's life and provide a continuing source of satisfaction. A coach can make a difference.

College Coaching

College coaching provides high prestige. With this increased status and recognition come significantly greater pressure for success as well as exposure to controversy.

At the major colleges, head coaches command excellent salaries and fringe benefits, have a number of assistant coaches and staff, and frequently have additional opportunities for extra income. Some endorse products, have their own radio or television programs, give presentations, and conduct summer sports camps.

Head coaches of minor sports and coaches at smaller colleges do not enjoy such attention and income. Some are content, not wishing to exchange their situation for the pressure of the limelight.

Often head coaches at smaller schools teach physical education courses, though some teach academic subjects, or have other responsibilities on campus. They may work in the school's admissions office, direct the intramural program, or serve as assistant coach in other sports.

In addition to having coaching ability, the major college coach must have skills that enable her or him to deal with newspaper and television people. Good speaking qualities are essential, since coaches frequently speak at alumni meetings, athletic banquets, and community luncheons. Assistant coaches help with many aspects of the job, including one particularly important aspect—recruiting—aiding the head coach with her or his duties.

Much of a college coach's time is spent in convincing young persons to attend her or his college. In many situations, the coach's job relies on a consistent flow of good talent. Unfortunately, this has resulted in abuses in which players have been offered "deals" in violation of the rules that are set up by governing associations such as the NCAA and NAIA. Unfortunately, these scandals have cast a cloud over college sports.

If big-time college coaching doesn't sound attractive, don't despair. Many jobs exist at the community (junior) college and small college level. These offer the opportunity to achieve some recognition locally while deriving many of the benefits of coaching.

What opportunities exist for women? A fantastic number of situations are available at the college level for women. Just as women's opportunities have expanded in school coaching, many women's college positions now exist. In fact, several colleges have strongly emphasized women's sports, playing a major schedule of games, publicizing the team, and extensively recruiting student/athletes for scholarships. By law (Title IX) women must have the same opportunities as men. All schools offer women's sports programs; most employ part-time coaches who may have other positions at the college or who derive their main income from private business. Michelle Sharp, head women's coach at Manhattan University in New York City, typifies this situation. She serves as both faculty member and coach, teaching physical education and coaching women's basketball and softball.

Since colleges vary in terms of size and sports emphasis, those considering a coaching career have a wide range of schools from which to choose. Consequently, you should be able to mesh your personal interests with the college of your choice.

PROFESSIONAL COACHING

Professional coaching is generally more pressure-packed than big time college coaching. At this level, fewer opportunities exist, but those that do provide excellent salaries, benefits, and supportive staffs. If in reading these chapters you have come to the conclusion that directing athletic teams is extremely time-consuming, you are absolutely correct. Furthermore, at all levels, successful coaches work to improve themselves not only during preseason and the season, but throughout the entire year. This is particularly true of those managing professional teams.

At this stage, job security is most precarious; few seasons pass in which several coaches are not replaced. Persons at this level rarely remain with one team for an entire career. Coaches become more expendable than players.

In addition to handling the normal chores common to all in this position, the technique of motivating highly paid athletes remains a challenge. Coach-player relationships are particularly important in this regard. Gene Shue, former general manager and one of the most respected coaches in basketball, believes that coaches should not be "buddy-buddy" with players. He prefers time away from the team, though he likes to know what they're doing. But he does not want to be a baby-sitter. At the lower levels, in school settings, coaches often serve in the capacity of a father.

Most professional coaches have not only assistants but also specialists such as an athletic trainer and a health and strength coach; in addition, they frequently use the services of a scouting organization to evaluate college prospects.

The professional coach serves under the team's general manager and is also responsible to the owner. In most cases, they work as a unit on decisions regarding players such as trades and acquisitions.

Professional coaches usually come from the college ranks, although most usually gain experience as assistants on professional teams before moving to the top post. In addition to excellent salaries (most in major sports earn over $200,000 a year), many opportunities exist to supplement their income. While pro coaching openings occur often, only highly skilled and usually well-known coaches are considered for these positions. If you wish to make it to the ranks of a professional coach, years of preparation and an excellent record of success will be necessary, and this in no way guarantees the job. In some cases, experience as a professional player will help.

Considerable hoopla surrounds professional sports teams and no one can discount the glamour, the prestige, or the satisfaction of earned success. Media attention focuses no brighter anywhere in America than on winning professional coaches, nor does so little sympathy exist for a deposed loser. Fortunately, many of the skills necessary in coaching, such as organizational ability and skill in working with people, are useful in the business world. Consequently, most ex-pro coaches find employment in sales, public relations, and management. Others return to teaching while retaining an involvement in their sport by serving part-time as scouts. A fortunate few find careers as sports announcers.

The interest in sports shows no sign of slowing—there will be a continuing need for the few who make it to the select group designated as professional coaches.

VOLUNTEER COACH

Many neighborhood, church, and community teams rely upon volunteers to coach teams of young people. Little League baseball, Babe Ruth softball, PAL, Pop Warner Football, YMCA, YMHA, YWCA, YWHA, CYO, Optimist, JCC, and many similar groups could not serve the millions of players without the free services of many coaches. While some receive a salary, usually it is very little when the amount of time is considered. While the income may be none or little, the responsibility remains great—most often it is here that children receive their first experience at organized sports.

In recent years it has become fashionable to criticize the abuses and mistakes of volunteer coaches. While some of this is clearly justified—a few coaches have overemphasized winning, some need improved organizational skills and others have underemphasized development of players—the vast majority of volunteer coaches make a substantial contribution.

Acting as a volunteer coach can serve as an enjoyable outlet while you benefit others. Unfortunately, many take on the job with little information about the role and only superficial knowledge of the sport. In some cases, awkward solutions have occurred because of improper handling of behavior problems or an injury.

It is extremely important for any coach working with youngsters to prepare herself or himself for the assignment. Fred Engh of the Athletic Institute, a specialist on young people's programs, feels that youngsters notice how a coach dresses and talks, handles emotion, uses fair standards, and knows the rules of the sport. Engh also points out that coaches can be held liable for any physical harm incurred by players in their charge.

Coaching is basically teaching, and good coaches build not only good athletes but also good citizens.

PREPARING TO COACH

If you're planning a career as a coach, the time to begin is now.

The following abilities have been listed by the American Association for Health, Physical Education and Recreation as necessary for the prospective coach. In preparing for your career, these serve as helpful guidelines:

1. An understanding of the relationship of the interscholastic program and the particular sport you are coaching to the total education program.
2. A knowledge of first aid and the safety practices and techniques pertinent to the sport you are coaching.
3. An understanding of the possibilities of legal liability as well as sound practices and preventive measures.
4. A thorough knowledge and understanding of the biological, social, moral, emotional, and spiritual values that may accrue

from the activity and the best methods of bringing about these desirable outcomes.

5. A knowledge of the most acceptable principles of growth and development and their implications for the sport.
6. An understanding of the basic principles in the care and prevention of injuries together with an understanding of the proper relationship of the coach to the school or team physician.
7. An understanding of the best methods of developing and conditioning members of athletic squads.
8. The ability to speak in public to bring credit to the profession and the school and to more effectively inform the public of the educational possibilities of the sport.
9. An understanding of the basic psychological principles of motivation, stress, play, and group interaction.
10. A thorough knowledge of the fundamentals, offenses, defenses, strategies, and teaching methods involved in a particular sport. Included will be squad organization, coaching techniques, and sound motivational procedures.
11. A knowledge and sense of responsibility for local, state, and national rules.

If you go to college to become a physical education teacher, you should achieve all of the above. Studying another program at college or not attending means you will need to prepare yourself.

The following list offers suggestions for *all* those wishing to enter the ranks of the profession:

1. Participate in sports. If you are unable to compete at the varsity level, play on intramural and community teams.
2. Attend practices of several teams at various levels to observe coaches' organization and teaching technique. This is important not only for nonathletes but also those who have participated in sports. It's easy to fall into the trap of "coaching the way you were coached."

3. Observe as many games, matches, meets as you can. While doing so, become a student of the sport. Observe how a coach performs her or his magic or makes a mistake. For example, in basketball how does the coach use time outs, in hockey how are substitutions handled, in football what adjustments are made at half time, or in baseball exactly when is a relief pitcher brought in to replace the starter? Quite often the difference between a fan and one studying a game is that the fan only watches the main action (usually the ball) while the keen observer watches the behavior of the other players and the actions of the coach.

4. Study the rules and rule changes of your sport so that as coach you will be knowledgeable in using the rules for your benefit and that of your team. Strategy frequently revolves around the rules of the game, with opposing coaches working to gain an advantage.

5. Select some coaches whom you admire and use them as models for yourself. You may want to write and ask them to share some of their materials with you. Many coaches will provide information on their approaches to the sport, including specifics in areas such as practice organization and weight training. A coaching model need not have a fantastic record; many coaches are very good yet have only mediocre win-loss histories.

6. Discover what functions sports officials, scorekeepers, statisticians, and athletic directors perform at an athletic event. If you do not have athletic ability, you may wish to volunteer to serve as a manager or statistician for a team. One of the best ways to gain an excellent close-up feel of athletics is to serve as a referee, judge, or umpire. Not only does this enable you to practice instant recall of the rules but gain an insight into the flow of the event. Frequently, lower-level sports teams go begging for officials. Volunteer; it will make you a better coach.

7. Investigate the off-season techniques to develop players in your sport. For example, weight training equipment and procedures, conditioning, visual enhancement, and nutrition have changed

dramatically in recent years. Future coaches should stay informed about these developments. Observe athletes and their coaches in working situations during the off-season.

8. Attend professional meetings, conferences, and clinics and join the coaching associations related to your sports interest.

Membership in the following organizations is strongly encouraged:

National Youth Sports Coaches Association
1509 North Military Trail
West Palm Beach, FL 33409

National High School Athletic Coaches Association
3423 E. Silver Springs Blvd., Suite 9
Ocala, FL 32670

National Association of Basketball Coaches (College)
9300 W. 110th Street
Suite 640
Overland Park, KS 66210

National Association for Girls and Women in Sports
1900 Association Drive
Reston, VA 22091

National Federation of Interscholastic Coaches
11724 NW Plaza Circle
Kansas City, MO 64195

9. Develop a collection of instructional videotapes and a library of books, articles, and clippings on coaching the sport of your interest. In particular, read the following magazines: *The Coaching Clinic, Scholastic Coach,* and the *Athletic Journal.* Consult also the publications for coaching youth leagues published by the Athletic Institute. Books range form *Modern Athletic Training* and *Basketball—The Women's Game* to the videos "Your Total Guide to Strength and Conditioning" and "The ESPN Youth

Coaching" series. Sports Videos (745 State Circle, Ann Arbor, MI 48106) provide a large collection from which to select; samples include: "The Science of Pitching," "Tom Tutko's Coaching Clinic," and "Sports Psychology for Youth Coaches."
10. Volunteer to serve as assistant coach for a team of children in your community. This will give you the experience as well as the opportunity to learn and experiment in developing your own coaching philosophy and ideas.

Coaching can be one of the most positive and wholesome careers our society has to offer. In order to realize these benefits, a tremendous commitment of time and energy will be needed and the earlier you begin the better. If you think it may not be worth it, consider the following taken from an article entitled "Thoughts about My Coach" from the magazine, *Young Athlete:*

> Back in the early 1920's, when I was in the seventh grade at West Orange, New Jersey's Fairmont Middle School I met a man who changed my whole life.
> His name was Lawrence Quallo, our athletic director. . . . As a youngster I was not a very good athlete, but I did my best. Then one day on the basketball court, after I had been lucky enough to score, Mr. Quallo stopped the game, came over to me and asked, "Eddie, would you like to try out for our team? . . . I think you have the makings of a good player."
> Thanks to Larry Quallo's influence, I went on to become a fairly good three-letter man in high school. So much did Larry inspire and guide me that, when I was in my junior year of high school, I scored over 1,000 points for the basketball team (I missed only one foul shot), scored 11 touchdowns and ran the hundred in 10 seconds flat. I tried to please Larry. My reward? He said he was more than pleased. That was enough . . .
> I'm now in the Hall of Fame, but only because of Larry. He helped my dreams come true. He put a real foundation under my dreams, insuring they'd become reality. He was like a father to me, and I bless his memory every day of my life.

CHAPTER 3

SPORTS ADMINISTRATION

"People said I was crazy. Hey, I was going to NFL. Little did they know when I got there I'd be working for nothing." The year, 1977; the person, Charlie Casserly. Today he serves as general manager for the Washington Redskins NFL football team!

Casserly had a dream—working in the National Football League. He wrote to every team expressing that desire—coach George Allen hired him as an unpaid intern. He left his high school teaching and football coaching position and has never regretted it. Fortunately he had the opportunity to work with super coach George Allen and Bobby Baethard, combining on-the-job training with his own abilities and knowledge of football. After serving in several capacities, today he is an executive for one of sport's most successful franchises.

The explosive growth of athletics has created a serious need for individuals to manage and direct school, college, professional, and organizational programs. The latter category includes everything from the Blockbuster Football Bowl, to McDonald's High School All American Basketball Game and the Iron Man Triathlon. Competent leadership provides proper organization to each detail, resulting in success for the participant, school/organization and, if relevant, the sponsor.

SCHOOL ATHLETIC DIRECTOR

Universities, colleges, community colleges, high schools, junior highs, and middle schools (and even some elementary schools) utilize the services of an athletic director (AD). These men and women follow career patterns similar to O'Neil High School (Highland Falls, NY) AD Gerry Kaplan. He came to his present school as a basketball coach and physical education teacher. Upon the retirement of the previous AD he was appointed by the board of education to his position. Presently in addition to his teaching duties as physical educator, he coaches the varsity basketball team and serves as AD. He teaches his classes in the early part of the day, leaving the afternoon free for administrative duties—scheduling, attending meetings, coordinating intramurals, etc. At smaller schools the AD will teach a couple of classes; at larger schools the position will command full-time attention.

Athletic directors feel like Larry Hazel (retired), North Chicago (Illinois) High School. He enjoyed the challenge of being athletic director, conducted a well-organized program, and worked for a conference championship in all sports. Larry coordinated the activities of several sports and coaches; for example, during the fall, 15 teams participate in interscholastic sports!

If Hazel's position sounds demanding, consider the athletic director at the University of Texas who lists among his duties the following areas—business office (tickets, concessions); sports information; trainers and equipment manager; coaches; athletic dining hall; and stadium supervision. The Texas AD has an assistant and secretarial support; this is common at the major universities. The position varies with the size of the school or college. Recently many colleges (and some schools) have added a director or coordinator of women's athletics. And don't overlook the growing opportunities afforded by the community college.

Salaries range in the category of $35,000 to $70,000 per year for school athletic directors, with duties that vary widely. Some college positions exceed $100,000. The salary is for twelve months of work, as opposed to the ten-month commitment of teachers.

Some professional organizations list the abilities necessary in athletic administrators. These include an understanding of:

1. The role of athletics in education and our society and the rules, regulations, policies, and procedures of the various governing bodies.
2. Sound business procedures as related to athletic administration.
3. Administrative problems as related to equipment and supplies.
4. Problems related to facilities, indoor and outdoor.
5. School law and liability.
6. The factors involved in the conduct of athletic events.
7. Good public relations techniques.
8. Staff relationships.
9. The health aspects of athletics.
10. The psychological and sociological aspects of sports.

Reuben Frost, Director of Health, Physical Education and Recreation Division, Springfield College, believes the successful athletic director requires many important personality qualities:

1. Leadership
2. A sincere interest in youth and their development
3. A sense of humor
4. Even temperament
5. Optimism
6. A sense of justice and impartiality
7. Integrity and solidarity

Richard Borkowski, Ed.D., athletic director at the Episcopal Academy (Merion, PA) to the list adds, "in this era more than ever, marked by a severe shortage of quality coaches, development of coaches must rank high on any list of the skills of ADs. This would include everything from conditioning and practice organization through injury prevention, player development, and safety procedures."

Public school administrators need certification to hold their positions; this requires specialized graduate work. In addition, the following organization provides a Certified Athletic Administrator (CAA) program.

National Federation of State High School Associations
11724 NW Plaza Circle
Kansas City, MO 64195

The AD sits at the top of the sports management triangle—a position that both challenges and rewards those who hold it.

PROFESSIONAL AND OTHER POSITIONS

On May 9, 1991, Abe Pollin, Chairman of the Board of the Washington Bullets, made sports history. He announced the appointment of Susan O'Malley as the president of the team; she became the first female ever to hold such a position. Pollin later commented, "I didn't realize that appointing a woman to run a team had never been done before. But she deserved it."

O'Mally, with a background in advertising, made her mark in sports while in a number of positions with the Bullets. In the forefront of sports marketing in the 90s, she improved season ticket sales and paid attendance significantly. In addition she has negotiated expanded radio contracts for the team and financially lucrative sponsorships for courtside advertising. She has moved ahead because of her understanding of the direction of sports and her ability to capitalize on her skills and knowledge for the team's benefit. Those interested in sports management must absolutely understand and implement modern sports marketing to be a success in the future.

Numerous opportunities exist for positions of administration in nonschool situations. Not all of these are top-level positions; many people serve in supportive roles directing specific aspects of a program. For example, most professional baseball teams have officials comparable to the New York Mets. The team has a Director of Player Development, a

Promotions Director, a Director of Minor League Operations, and similar positions.

Many athletic conferences have full-time administrators. Mike Tranghese serves the relatively new Big East Conference as commissioner. His position commands a salary of over $100,000 per year! He has gained an excellent reputation for negotiating television contracts, a skill necessary at his level, and developing Big East football.

The Big Ten Conference employs a Commissioner, two Assistant Commissioners, and four other persons in lower-level administrative positions. Similarly the National Collegiate Athletic Association, under its Executive Director, employs a large staff. A sampling of these positions are Director of Promotion, Director of Enforcement, Assistant Director of Events, and Director of Publishing. The President's Council on Physical Fitness and Sports enjoys the services of Director of Information, Federal-State Relations, Program Development and Community Programs, and Special Projects.

The obvious question: how does one obtain a position in sports administration such as those above? People arrive in such positions in a variety of ways; historically, most have gone the administration route: that is, obtaining a position at a lower level and working their way to the top. Gil Swalls, Assistant Director, Big Ten Service Bureau, Big Ten Conference, is already off to a good start. Still in his twenties, his background includes a B.S. in Radio-Television from Southern Illinois University; and while in college he served in the sports information office, on the school newspaper, and on the school radio station. In addition, he worked part-time for several newspapers. Upon graduation he was hired by the Big Ten.

In the future most persons in this field will enter not only because of their on-the-job experience but also because of their education. Administrative expertise in organization, budgeting, communication (written and oral), and human relations will still remain very important, but specific knowledge obtained in course work will increase in significance.

EDUCATION

Many colleges offer sports management and leadership programs. One of the first, the University of Massachusetts, offers an excellent program in Sport Management at the undergraduate and graduate levels. Students take courses such as the following:

Structure and Function of Sport Organizations
History of Sport in the U.S.
Sport Marketing and Management
Seminar in Sport Management
Managerial Analysis for Sport Organization

According to the student's area of specialization, additional courses are taken from the School of Business Administration, the School of Education, and the School of Hotel, Restaurant, and Travel Administration. The Structure and Functions in Sport Organizations, an important course in the program, has two main purposes: 1) to contribute to the body of knowledge related to structure and functions within the various sport organizations, and 2) to guide the student in the development of an in-depth study on some aspect of sport management. Perhaps the most interesting course, entitled The Internship, involves a field experience in which the student works in a full-time situation in an area of choice; for example, professional team sports, collegiate athletics, and other sports areas. Graduates have obtained positions in many areas such as the following:

College Instructor	Director of Public Relations
Sporting Goods Sales	Wrestling Coach
High School Instructor	Athletic Coach
Assistant Coach-Football	Athletic Director
Recreation Supervisor	Ass't Director, Public Relations
Manager, Tennis Club	

Another program of interest, Sports Administration at the University of Miami (in Florida) has attracted considerable attention. "The program for persons interested in Athletic Sports administration or Recreation and Leisure Sports Administration" leads to a master's degree. The following courses constitute part of the program:

Organization and Administration of Sports Programs
Fiscal Management in Sports Administration
Legal Aspects of Sports and Exercise Science

Additional requirements and electives round out the program.

Legal liability area has increasing importance to all those in sports and specifically to those in athletic management. Knowledge of legal issues and risk management is a must. College courses reflect this concern; these readings are suggested:

Law and Liability in Athletics, Physical Education, and Recreation. (Allyn and Bacon, Publisher).

Principles of Safety in Physical Education and Sport. (American Alliance for Health, Physical Education, Recreation and Dance, Publisher).

Safety in School—Sports and Fitness. (J. Weston Walch, Publisher).

Clearly, positions in sports administration look attractive. But don't overlook the amount of work involved in such jobs. Long hours and weekend commitments appear as a common schedule, but the people enjoy what they are doing so much they do not consider it work!

"I love my job. I serve as Associate Athletic Director at Yale University. We offer a wide range of sports (from a squash squad to an equestrian team!); similarly our intramural program provides opportunities from aerobics to women's flag football," explains Larry Matthews, Ed.D. Clearly you must enjoy working with young people to serve in school sports management; in addition, you should try for employment at a school or college that emphasizes your sport(s). If you love wrestling—you should apply for positions at schools that have a wrestling tradition.

If sports management interests you, consult your school counselor for college programs and participate in sports in some capacity (player, student manager/trainer, school paper sports writer) and when possible, observe athletic administrators in their roles. Study sporting events from the perspective of management (scheduling and paying of the officials). Volunteer to assist at these games and contests.

The following materials provide valuable information for present and future sports management personnel.

Athletic Administrators Reference Manual
National Interscholastic Athletic Administration Association
P.O. Box 20626
Kansas City, MO 64195

American Alliance for Health, Physical Education, Recreation
and Dance
1900 Association Drive
Reston, VA 22091
(state affiliates provide information also; student memberships exist)

Athletic Business (periodical)
1842 Hoffman St. Suite 201
Madison, WI 53704

Athletic Institute's *Sports and Physical Education* (catalog)
200 Castlewood Drive
North Palm Beach, FL 33408–5697

Sports Address Bible (an annual)
Global Sports Productions
1223 Broadway, Suite 101
Santa Monica, CA 90404

Sports Market Place
Sportswide
P.O. Box 1417
Princeton, NJ 08542

CHAPTER 4

SPORTS OFFICIATING

"What is the number one attribute of a good sports official?"
"The gift of a sense of humor is above everything else. I believe
it should be on the top of every official's list regardless of the sport
he or she works."

Tom Kline
Veteran college and high school sports official,
quoted in *Referee Magazine*

Sure, everyone loves being close to the game—down on the court,
out on the field—but only a few can do it as an official. This career
clearly tests the character, energy, knowledge, skills, and fitness of the
participants as they make split-second decisions.

For many years officiating was considered a thankless job where the
official took verbal abuse and occasionally physical abuse from the
coach, players, and crowd. More recently, a growing respect has been
noticeable at all levels for the men and women who make the game work
by enforcing the rules. This has probably occurred because of a growing
militancy on the part of the officials, an increase in their skills, and a
realization of their importance and dedication by the public.

A strong movement exists within the profession of officiating to
continually upgrade performance quality of officials. Consequently at
the college level mandatory clinics exist in many Division I sports; at
the school level growing numbers of states have begun to require

attendance at a training camp to be eligible to work a state tournament game. For example, the Board of Control of the Kentucky High School Athletic Association has a program requiring all high school baseball umpires to attend a one-day training session if they wish to receive consideration to officiate in the state's tournament games. Undoubtedly as this movement spreads to many states, officials will gain a further increase in status, salaries will rise, and the career will attract additional potential members.

Ninety-five percent of all officials serve on a part-time basis working mainly with schools, colleges, semiprofessional teams, and recreation leagues.

Skippy Kingwill, New Jersey sports official, typifies most high school officials. During the day he teaches at the elementary level at the Horace Mann School in the town of North Bergen. At the end of the school day he leaves for the game he has been assigned to as referee or umpire. During the winter months he works men's and women's basketball and volleyball games and in the spring, women's and men's softball. Many officials earn their livelihood as educators, others own their own businesses or work flexible hours in careers such as sales so as to be available for afternoon sporting events.

While most view the profession as an avocation, a select few make it to the circle of full-time professional officials. These individuals normally "pay their dues" by obtaining several years of experience at the lower levels such as high school, college, and the minor leagues. Richie Powers, in his fine book, *Overtime* (published by Ballantine) provides an excellent look at the life of a professional basketball official in the National Basketball Association. He states,

> I'm usually quick with the whistle and even quicker with my thumb, in the area of technical fouls, but I set a record tonight by calling my first technical of the season less than two minutes into the game. Manny (Sokol) had called a foul against Phil Chenier of the Bullets. Instead of rolling the ball to Manny, or at least bouncing it toward him, Chenier held it defiantly, glaring in Manny's direction. Then he flipped the ball out of bounds. Tweet!

I hit him with a technical foul for unsportsmanlike conduct . . .
Listen, I call technical fouls in an attempt to maintain control of
the game.

Quite obviously, the emotional control of officials is tested many
times in each game.

OFFICIATING GUIDELINES

Veteran official Tom Kline believes using humor "can diffuse a
potentially volatile situation as a reminder that we are involved in a game
that should be kept in proper perspective." In addition, the following
guidelines have been prepared by *Referee Magazine*.

Be Competitive—The players give maximum effort, so should
you. Tell yourself, "I'm not going to let this game get away from
me, I am better than that." You are hired to make the calls that
control the game—make them!

Have Your Head on Right—Don't think your striped shirt grants
you immunity from having to take a little criticism. It's part of
officiating. Plan on it. Successful officials know how much to
take. Ask one when you get the chance.

Don't Be a Tough Guy—If a coach is on your back but not
enough to warrant a penalty, then stay away from him (or her).
This is especially true during time outs. Standing near an unhappy
coach just to "show him" will only lead to further tensions. Some
officials develop irritating characteristics. Don't be one of them.

Get into the Flow of the Game—Each game is different. Good
officials can feel this difference. Concentrate on the reactions of
the players. Take note if the tempo of the game changes. A ragged
game calls for a different style of officiating from a smooth one.

Don't Bark—If you don't like to be shouted at, don't shout at
someone else. Be firm but with a normal, relaxed voice. This
technique will do wonders in helping you to reduce the pressure.
Shouting indicates a loss of control—not only of one's self, but
also of the game.

Show Confidence—Cockiness has absolutely no place in officiating. You want to exude confidence. Your presence should command respect from the participants. As in any walk of life, appearance, manner, and voice determine how you are accepted. Try to present the proper image.

Forget the Fans—As a group, fans exhibit three characteristics: ignorance of the rules, highly emotional partisanship, and delight in antagonizing the officials. Accepting this fact will help you ignore the fans, unless they interrupt the game or stand in the way of your doing your job.

Answer Reasonable Questions—Treat coaches and players in a courteous way. If they ask you a question reasonably, answer them in a polite way. If they get your ear by saying, "Hey, Ref, I want to ask you something," and then start telling you off, interrupt and remind them of the reason for the discussion. Be firm, but relaxed.

Choose Your Words Wisely—Don't obviously threaten a coach or players. This will only put them on the defensive. More importantly, you will have placed yourself on the spot. If you feel a situation is serious enough to warrant a threat, then it is serious enough to penalize, without invoking a threat. Obviously some things you say will be a form of threat, but using the proper words can make it subtle.

Stay Cool—Your purpose is to establish a calm environment for the game. Nervous or edgy officials are easily spotted by fans, coaches, and players alike. Avoid chewing gum, pacing around, or displaying a wide range of emotions prior to or during a game; this will serve to make you seem vulnerable to the pressure.

The above suggestions, generally applicable to officiating at all levels, may need slight modification in special situations. However, as a whole they provide excellent guidelines. Richard Schafer, Assistant Director, National Federation of State High School Associations, believes that excellent mechanics and a thorough knowledge of the rules are an important part of being a truly successful official. But establishing and maintaining rapport with coaches and players alike will help the official avoid many potentially difficult situations.

One researcher, Dr. Roy Askins, a professor of social psychology who officiates part-time, has examined his hobby and provides the following information. When asked "What gives officials the most trouble?" Dr. Askins said that other than problems associated with perception and sloppy play, the behavior of some coaches, players, and crowds is most troublesome.

At this point you may ask, "If officiating is so demanding in terms of working conditions, why do people do it?" Dr. Askins's survey found many reasons. The most common are earning extra money, remaining close to athletics in some capacity, and enjoying a position of some status and power. If you think this career looks promising for you, make plans to begin.

GETTING STARTED

What kind of person makes a good sports official? Dr. R. C. Haygood, a vocational psychologist at Arizona State University, says that the ideal sports official is a *saint*. Only a saint could exhibit all of the psychological traits we expect of a good referee or umpire. Some of these personality characteristics are tolerance, self-confidence, and the ability to make decisions under stress; there's one way to see if you possess these: give officiating a try.

Volunteer to officiate intramurals at your school or college, in a church or synagogue league in your neighborhood, or in the community recreation program. Your involvement can aid yourself and the league; some youth leagues and intramural programs even will provide salaries but your greatest benefit will be experience. In addition, officiating is an excellent way to better understand a sport; it will give you a better appreciation of the total game as well as a working knowledge of the rules. This serves as a valuable background for careers as professional athletes and coaches.

If you become seriously interested, it's useful to remember that officiating parallels coaching in many respects. That is, novices work with younger players at the lower level. So following approval, you will usually work games at the junior high school and the junior varsity level. In order to receive initial status it will be necessary to pass a written examination in the sport or sports of your choice and to join the state association and the local chapter.

Many leagues go begging for officials—Who's going to ref college intramurals? Who's going to ref the winter Optimist basketball league? Who's going to ref the neighborhood girl's softball teams?—and choose rookies, novices, and beginners. Many leagues cannot attract or afford certified officials; this provides you opportunities. The door is wide open for women.

"I love it. It works well with my life-style and family obligations, and I enjoy the physical activity and the income it provides," says Peggy Kershner McKernan. Peggy, one of the first women to officiate men's basketball in Florida, presently lives in Pennsylvania and works high school and college games on the East Coast. In addition, she lectures and works with beginning refs at camps and clinics.

In many ways Peggy personifies the emergence of women in athletics. She has entered a previously all-male dominion and has had success. She feels the officiating works well for her, normally refereeing in the evenings when her husband can stay with their children. It has worked out as a perfect part-time job.

During the probationary period, usually a couple of years, the newcomer will come under the observation of senior officials for evaluation. They will look for a good working knowledge of the game, combined with several abilities, for example, how does he or she perform in a stressful situation? As new officials improve their skills they will be asked to work more games and be promoted to higher-level games, perhaps even an important tournament or championship event. Naturally, salaries improve with the level officiated and with geographic location; most have improved significantly in recent years.

Some officials will want to move on to the college level. This will involve joining another association, taking a test, and proving oneself again. College officials receive excellent per-game salaries and most conferences also pay travel expenses.

One major college conference listed its requirements: Applicants for officials' positions should be less than forty years of age when applying, in good physical condition, and able to pass an exam. These characteristics and three ability references must be submitted and, while a high school diploma is necessary, a college degree is preferred. In addition, the person must have employment and residence in close proximity to the conference. The candidate's job has to permit flexibility so as to be free for travel and games. While some background as a player is desirable, the officiating experience must include: eight to ten years at the high school level; four to ten years at the community college and/or four-year college level; approximately four years in a compatible conference. If the above criteria appear too demanding, remember that most positions will not be this difficult to obtain—the above requirements represent a special situation for one of the nation's premier conferences.

OFFICIATING SCHOOLS

Although a study of the readership of *Referee Magazine* indicates that most officials became introduced to their profession by a friend or through participation in sports, many future officials will probably enter their careers as a result of attendance at a school. Naturally, the official's associations will provide a training program for their new recruits; the schools, however, represent an in-depth concentrated approach to learning the officials' art. Some master officials conduct annual conferences for officials. These clinics (usually two-day meetings) exist for officials of all levels who wish to improve their skills.

The following serve as typical examples of the schools available. The Harry Wendelstedt School for Umpires, as its name implies, educates baseball umpires. The specific purpose is to supply supervised training for young people to qualify for umpire positions in professional, college, high school, semipro, and sandlot baseball. The school, which meets for six weeks, runs from directly after the New Year's holiday until early February. The program follows this schedule. Classes begin at 8:30 with a ninety-minute session that explains and tests the student's knowledge of the rules and situations which actually confront umpires. At 10:30 the class reports to the playing fields. A program of exercises and conditioning takes place. Following this, a series of practice drills takes place to teach proper mechanics—stance, voice control, positions, and others. Each student receives instruction and practice in all phases of umpiring. After the completion of the first ten days of school, the late afternoons, 3:30 until 6:00, are spent working high school and college games. Naturally no jobs are promised, but many, many of the graduates have entered the profession at all levels. Some (approximately 15) exceptional students do receive appointments directly after finishing the school, and many are called at a later date. This school has trained the majority of the men in blue working in the majors today. If this sounds interesting, for additional information write:

Harry Wendelstedt School for Umpires
    88 South Street Andrews Drive
    Ormond Beach, FL 32074

Each summer Nationwide Basketball Referee Camp hosts many active and aspiring officials at its programs in Pennsylvania, Georgia, and Indiana. The three-day session attracts persons from all over the country. The camp format begins with morning presentations, films, and lectures. Topics such as Floor Mechanics, What Type of Officials Supervisors Look for at the Higher Levels, The Personality Traits of Successful Officials, and The Proper Use of Signals form some of the content of the course.

Following lunch, the refs work games of high school players attending a nearby camp. Each one receives an evaluation of the game he or she officiates. Evenings find the students actively officiating; each ref participates in four games daily. At the conclusion of camp, each person receives an honest appraisal of her or his ability. The refs attend to expand their knowledge and skills with the hope they can improve the level of games they work. Many do profit and "move up"; others may need improvement that will come through experience. If you wish additional information, contact:

Nationwide Basketball Referee's Camp
  4520 Jolyn Place
  Atlanta, GA 30342

Ron Applegate directs the Michigan State Midwest Officials Camp in East Lansing specifically designed for aspiring college women's basketball referees. "My camp is an exposure camp—people who have aspirations of moving to Division I women's basketball officials are the people we attract." Exposure camps emphasize the highlighting talents of an official on the way up while providing some training. Most camps, clinics, or schools emphasize both.

While most clinics provide active sessions with officials working games, some lecture-discussion sessions exist. The National Association of Sports Officials Convention offers numerous sessions in a variety of sports. These serve to update and orient officials to rule changes, points of emphasis, and resolution of potential problems that may occur. They may be contacted at:

NASO
  2017 Lathrop Avenue
  Racine, WI 53405

The American Softball Association offers its ASA National Umpire schools around the nation; they provide advanced sessions also. Interested persons should contact:

American Softball Association
  2801 NE 50th Street
  Oklahoma City, OK 73111

Opportunities exist in all areas for officials, but particularly in women's sports and certain minor sports. Salaries range widely; most officials earn approximately $80 per game for high school major varsity sports and $100 (with major conferences paying significantly more) at the college level. Tournaments and championship games command more money. Professional salaries will vary with the sport and the number of games. Baseball umpires average $100,000 per year for their full-time jobs; boxing officials receive a per-event salary.

The expansion of sports at all levels and the growth of women's participation guarantee opportunities for new officials. Dr. Henry Nichols, NCAA national coordinator of men's basketball, states, "We can always use good new ones; it's a great way to stay close to the game and competition and have a positive impact."

PREPARING FOR YOUR FUTURE

If officiating is potentially your career, pursue these suggestions:

1. Read about your future profession—subscribe to *Referee Magazine;* it contains excellent information, updates, current happenings, profiles of successful officials, and suggestions for improving. For a subscription, write:

   Referee Magazine
   P.O. Box 161
   Franksville, WI 53126

   Read the study books on officiating such as some recent books from *Referee Magazine: Case Book Plus—Volleyball; The Football Official's Answer Book; Take Charge! Baseball Umpiring* and some classic books on officiating: Richie Power's *Overtime* (Ballantine), John McDonough's *Don't Hit Him, He's Dead* (Celestial Arts), and Edward Dolan's *Calling the Play: A Beginner's Guide to Amateur Sports Officiating* (Atheneum).

   Eric Gregg's book, *Working the Plate: The Eric Gregg Story* (William Morrow), provides excellent insight into the life of an African-American umpire's rise from the minors to the big leagues. His comments apply to all officials regardless of race.

Pam Postema's *You Got To Have Balls To Make It In This League* (Simon and Schuster) details a woman's experience in the baseball world trying to make it to the major leagues.

2. As suggested earlier, volunteer to officiate, wherever you can find an opportunity. Many exist. What you don't earn in salary you will in experience.

3. Study and master the rules for your sport. Stay aware of recent changes, interpretations, and emphases. The NCAA provides rule books (see address in Appendix A).

4. Participate to the extent you are able in the sport of your interest.

5. Work to develop the personality traits of an official, such as independence, maturity, self-confidence, and a high moral character.

6. Study your sport and its officials. Use your imagination and make the calls. It will be good practice.

7. Write to the administrative office of the league you might like to officiate and ask the requirements so you can begin to prepare. Each league (at all levels) will have a person performing the task of supervising and assigning officials. For example, for professional baseball, contact:

Office for Baseball Umpire Development
P.O. Box A
225 Fourth Street
St. Petersburg, FL 33731

Remember, despite the criticism officials too frequently get, most fans, players, and coaches greatly appreciate their role. Typical is recent basketball Hall of Fame inductee Al McGuire, formerly of Marquette University, who served as one of the nation's most successful basketball coaches. Though he proclaims that nobody got on officials more than he did, he also thinks that no one has more respect for those dedicated people and the difficult, thankless job that they do so well.

This point is further echoed by Ron Luciano, former major league baseball umpire in his enjoyable *The Fall of the Roman Umpire* (Bantam). "Without skilled umpires, I knew, the game could not exist. Oh, players were important, I accepted that, but there were plenty of players—too many players as far as some umpires were concerned. But there were only a select few people with the knowledge and judgment required to control a major-league game."

CHAPTER 5

SPORTS JOURNALISM

How about controlling the airwaves with snappy sports talk, clever interviews and colorful caller comments—no, not in the tradition of Ron Barr, Chet Coppock, Craig Miller, Chris "Mad Dog" Russo, Howard "King" Eskin, Dave Quinn, Suzyn Waldman, and Larry Munson, but as a producer!

A whole world of activity exists behind the scenes of these shows— scheduling guests, screening calls, scripting commercials, arranging traffic and weather reports, updating news, and other related activities. Producers handle these.

Typical is Larry Maxwell, producer for "Sports Byline," an evening radio talk show hosted by Ron Barr and heard on over 100 stations in the United States and abroad. Larry handles guest bookings for the show. "In one day I may talk to Pam Postema, Reggie White, Bill Walton, and Bobby Hull! If you love sports this job is a fantasy."

After attending Fairleigh Dickinson in New Jersey for a year, Larry headed west and moved to the San Francisco Bay area. He entered the restaurant business and stayed ten years; his love of sports drove him to apply for a number of positions on sports talk shows. Finally he obtained a position as an intern doing all sorts of jobs on the show, and he was not paid! After a few months luck struck. A job as a producer opened and the national show picked up in listenership and stations. Larry was hired. "I love my job, my family loves my job; what

I like best is when my friends go to work they read the *Wall Street journal,* the business section of the local paper and interoffice memos— I read the sports pages!"

Sports talk radio employs a variety of personnel to support the show—sales executives, accountants, engineers, producers, executive producers, and of course the host. Some hosts perform more than one function. Craig Miller at KRLD in Dallas works as a news reporter weekdays but on weekends he takes to the airwaves with sports. Others such as Wally Hall write sports *(Arkansas Democrat–Gazette)* full time and do a TV sports talk show (KARK–NBC) once a week. With the expansion of cable television, sports talk, sometimes with viewer participation, has moved into the TV realm.

Radio show hosts vary from "in your face talk," to "mild commentary" by the broadcaster about the performance of local teams and players, interviews with interesting sports personalities, and telephone calls from listeners. This job requires excellent knowledge of many sports, as the broadcaster frequently is "on the spot," and is only for persons who really love athletics. Most off-time will often find broadcasters attending games, press conferences, station promotions, and team practices. In addition to their shows, some handle sports news for their station.

Some have college backgrounds, but others do not; many worked as print journalists and sports announcers, some did games on cable, played or coached athletics, and others worked at stations and got a break. Regardless of their route, when the bell rang they were ready.

NEWSPAPER SPORTSWRITING

Tony Leodora presently serves as sports editor of the Norristown (Pennsylvania) *Times Herald* newspaper. Following college Tony took a position in business, but was able to pursue his lifelong interest in sports through working part-time at the newspaper. On weekends he'd cover local events and write them up for the paper. Part-time newspaper writers are called stringers. Eventually Tony decided to go full time and upon the retirement of the editor he was promoted to that position.

Tony works an irregular schedule. Mornings find him in the office; the afternoons are free except when he has an interview or game to cover. The evenings find him covering an athletic event and then writing and wiring his story to the office. Tony loves his job. He gets excellent seats at all athletic events, meets regularly with professional stars and coaches, occasionally travels to events in other cities, and gets paid for it. But it's not all fun and games. There are many long days, and writing is hard but enjoyable work. And he can't forget that deadlines absolutely, absolutely have to be met.

For many years, some of the finest journalism has been found on the sports pages of America's papers. It is here that lively, fast-paced action writing appears. The size, circulation, and location of a paper will determine to a large degree the activities of the sports writers. The sports department of small-town newspapers normally has an editor and another writer and perhaps two part-timers who cover weekend events. Such a paper will rely upon the wire services (Associated Press, United Press) for major stories.

A large city daily may have a staff of ten; several of these will have a particular specialty such as golf, football, boxing, or the high school scene. While these persons would cover other events during the season, they would also write several articles a week related to their expertise.

Frequently, reporters work unusual hours and days. For example, much like Tony Leodora, those employed by a morning newspaper will usually work late afternoon and evening hours, usually five days a week, including Saturday and Sunday, if there's a Sunday edition. They would then have two weekdays off. Major papers will send a reporter along with the team to cover out-of-town stories—while this sounds glamorous, it frequently is time-consuming and hectic. Following the event, the writer will use his or her notes to prepare the article, looking for a particular angle or interesting aspect to highlight for reader appeal. The writer sends in the completed article and finally gets to sleep, usually about 2:00 a.m.

PREPARING FOR YOUR CAREER

Many opportunities exist on school and college newspapers to begin your career. If a vacancy does not exist in sports, take a position writing news; it will help you build your craft of writing and will aid you to make a switch to sports when an opening occurs.

There are a lot of free tickets, but newspapers are notorious for paying mediocre salaries to their professionals, and smaller papers pay even less. Of course, it's possible that you will gain a reputation and your own column and a substantial income. "Having a column" means your work appears regularly in the same location in the paper, usually under your photograph. In terms of your career, it marks your success as a sportswriter. Your column would be commentary, mixed with reporting.

Most writers also produce books as a sideline. This serves as a creative outlet for their talents as well as an additional source of income. A considerable market exists for sports books, and publishers look for manuscripts from newspaper people. Likewise, sports magazines look for feature articles; this is an excellent source of income for the writer and permits him or her to gain a wider audience.

At one time, reporters began their careers as copy aides helping around the office by performing clerical tasks. Having proven themselves reliable, they might be asked to join the staff as cub reporters. This would involve small, unspectacular assignments eventually leading up to important tasks. Today few start this way. Most attend college and pursue course work in the department or school of journalism or communication arts. Ask a school counselor for information on colleges with programs in these areas. If you plan such a career, include several courses in writing; grammar skills will be a necessity. You should also consider a strong background in the humanities and using your free electives in sports courses from the physical education program. Courses in photography will increase your chances of obtaining a job, particularly with smaller papers.

Jackie Lopin, sportswriter, suggests that while you're in your last two years of college you make an especially strong effort to land a summer or part-time job on the local newspaper; constant news experience is the key to becoming a good sportswriter. These experiences will greatly enhance your ability to obtain a full-time position following graduation.

In recent years, the expansion of television and radio coverage of sporting events has resulted in a modification of newspaper coverage. A decline in straight factual reporting and an increase in features has occurred. Not only does the reader want to know what happened, but such additional information as the condition of the player injured, who might be traded, and the likelihood of the success against the next opponent. Some outstanding features have resulted from careful excellent investigative research revealing serious abuses in sports. However, most are interviews with an athlete answering a series of questions about an aspect of her or his career.

Despite its outward appearance, the life of a newspaper person has its lonely side. In fact, one observer found that "creative loneliness" is an important characteristic of successful writers. After the big game or press conference, the hard work of writing, editing, and rewriting must be completed—and prior to the deadline!

A newspaper writer at this point in time has a very special obligation to society to remain vigilant for excesses that may destroy sports. Too frequently, athletes, coaches, and administrators have engaged for personal benefit in conduct detrimental to their own profession. Coaches have forced injured players to participate; athletic directors have condoned illegal recruiting; players have put their own importance above that of their team and their sport; youth league managers have played only to win; and coaches have publicly abused players for mistakes. Even parents pressure their children unduly to be superstars. It is here that the writer can make an important contribution.

The number of big city papers has diminished in recent years; however, many papers have expanded and many others begun in new locations. Opportunities exist for well-prepared and knowledgeable candidates. In considering this career, Jackie Lopin reminded us that sometimes it's glamorous, usually it's exciting, but *always* it's very hard work; even the writers considered the best in the country will tell you that it took years and years of dedicated effort to develop their craft.

SPORTSCASTER

"I broke in by going to magazines such as *Sports Illustrated* and *Women's Sports*. I said to myself, 'Even if I'm not on the air I can research and write articles.' For broadcast journalism you need to look into the history of events and understand personalities."

Donna de Varona
Television Sports Commentator

De Varona points out that, as with all other sports careers, you must pay the price; that is, earn the position which you wish to attain. She became a household word through writing and broadcast success.

The sports world gives as much attention to well-known sports personalities from the broadcast media as they do some athletes. The glamour usually surrounds the *television announcers* who have great visibility and excellent salaries.

Often the hard work and time-consuming nature of "show biz" sports careers goes unnoticed. Consider a day in the life of CNN Sports newscaster Fred Hickman on an easy day!

The day for me usually begins about 7 a.m. That's when I kiss my wife good morning, and take the dog out to pick up the newspapers. I read several to begin preparation . . . *The Atlanta Constitution, The Chicago Tribune, The New York Times*, the *Los Angeles Times*, and *USA Today*.

I scan all of these thoroughly to give myself a feel of the current sports affairs and the different slants journalists are taking on them around the country.

Then it's telephone time. I check in with my office. I check in with different sources I have about the nation. In my early days in news, they were called the 'beat calls,' and I've never quite lost the habit. I think it's a good one.

I can hit CNN about 4:30 p.m., which is when we have our nightly production meeting. My co-anchor and I sit in with the show producers and assignment editor to get up to speed on what's happening and lay out the 11:00 broadcast. This is generally a thirty-minute affair.

Next it's off to makeup about 5 p.m. before heading back down to the computer to get started on the on-air promos. I tape two per evening to be aired on all the Turner Networks.

I then am ready to begin writing the show by 7:15. I get the 'readers' out of the way as soon as possible so as to be able to devote as much time to watching the games I'm responsible for covering that night.

I am also still working the telephones, the wires, etc., standing by for breaking news and how the breaking news will change the show.

I am finished writing by 10:30 but . . . unfortunately, the games don't always want to end just on time. This means the show is transforming all the time, even while we are on the air.

At 11:30, the red light goes off and I head home to mama.

But, in parting, may I say there is no such thing as a 'typical' day in my working life. It's always different, always challenging and always a blessing to feel the satisfaction I get from performing my task. Wouldn't trade it for a million bucks.

Television announcers receive the best salaries and the greatest exposure to the public. They may be employed by a team or a station or both. Some serve as the sports person on the station's news program. As such, they cover many areas necessitating a good knowledge at least of the major sports. Although they may appear on the show only twice a day for four or five minutes, they spend most of the day preparing for their air time. Often this involves attending press conferences, interviewing players, and covering games. It's an exciting life that brings the sportscaster in close contact with the athletic world. Many try their hand at automobile racing, playing quarterback (in practice), and pitching batting practice as a promotion. This occurs to increase viewer interest and to expand the announcer's credibility as knowledgeable about sports. In addition to very good speaking ability, writing skills are also essential since sportscasters compose the information they announce.

Closely related to the television news position is that of the *radio newscaster.* Some major stations in larger cities will employ a full-time specialist in this area; however, at smaller stations the sports person will handle other news stories as needed and may even serve as a part-time salesperson, obtaining commercials to be aired on the station.

Sports announcers have captured the attention of the American public; whether it's Dan and Frank jousting during a Monday night football game, Vince in L.A. analyzing a strategy, or Peggy Fleming providing her special expertise on the Winter Olympics. Clearly one of the glamour careers within the sports industry, they generally fall into two categories: play-by-play or color specialists. The former generally explains each play as it occurs and its relationship to the overall game. The color person, usually a former player, provides insights to certain techniques and strategies the coach or athlete may employ; he or she will often provide amusing anecdotes about players. Most recently there has been an attempt to carefully put together a team of announcers that will complement each other's abilities and contribute to the listener's enjoyment of the game. Many hours are spent by the staff in preparing for a game or event. Reading of players' backgrounds, talking with coaching staffs, and meeting with public relations specialists help in this regard.

HOW TO BEGIN

Knowledge of sports and an excellent speaking voice form a very important prerequisite for the sportscaster's career; physical attractiveness looms important for the television positions. Donna de Varona cautions that you should have a sports and academic background; it's very hard for someone who has never played basketball or been on the line in a competitive sport to really understand the dynamics of athletics. Therefore, it is useful to take many of the same courses suggested for newspaper and public relations careers, such as writing, public speaking, sport studies, and physical education. Similarly, try to become involved in sports at some level of activity. Also, obtain a position writing for a school paper, on the college radio station, or a community newsletter. If you do not attend college (or even if you do), consider attending a technical school designed for those seeking radio and television careers. These centers offer short, intensive courses and aid in placement in jobs. If you wish additional information, contact the following organization with your request for a list of these schools in your area:

National Association of Trade and Technical Schools
2012 K Street, N.W.
Washington, DC 20006

Two programs of note provide training for the aspiring broadcasters. Bill Raftery, television sportscaster, each summer for one week offers his "Sports Broadcasting Camp." Participants gain practice in announcing and analyzing games and interviewing, and then obtain feedback on their performance. The camp also offers a sportswriting program directed by Jerry Izenberg, syndicated sports columnist. The sessions feature lectures and discussion along with writing activities and feedback. Interested persons should contact:

Mid-Court Associates
P.O. Box 2487
Bloomfield, NJ 07003

Another option features the Connecticut School of Broadcasting located in several states. This intense program offers courses in areas such as Announcing, Studio Operations, Commercial Interpretation, Broadcast Journalism, Copywriting, Audio Production, and Sports. Schools such as CSB provide lectures, hands-on training and practice, and career advisement for students. Contact the school at:

Connecticut School of Broadcasting
Radio Park
Farmington, CT 06032

Once you have obtained the necessary education, Keith Jackson of ABC-TV's "Wide World of Sports" provides this suggestion that if you want to be a television sportscaster, begin where you are comfortable.

You shouldn't be so eager to run for the big city when the smaller community affords the better learning experience.

Many, many opportunities exist at the thousands of radio and hundreds of television stations in North America. Here the novice hones her or his skills and learns the art of the professional. Some individuals so enjoy their jobs in small towns and cities that they stay and make it a career. Others will use this background as a springboard to the "big time."

For additional information on sports journalism contact:

National Association of Broadcasters
1771 N Street, N.W.
Washington, DC 20036

National Sportscasters and Sportswriters Association
P.O. Drawer 559
Salisbury, NC 28144

CHAPTER 6

PHYSICAL EDUCATION

Young people have always admired their physical education teachers; some have considered entering this career themselves and have asked, "What do I take in college if I want to be a 'gym teacher'?"

Rutgers University (New Brunswick, NJ) offers a variety of sports-related programs including Sports Management, Exercise Science, and Teaching Physical Education. Students in the latter option take general courses (General Psychology, Human Anatomy, college requirements, and electives); sports-related courses (Sports and the Law, Exercise Physiology, and others); and courses related to physical education teaching (Instructional Design in Physical Education, Teaching and Coaching Individual Sports, Seminar in Physical Education Teaching, Student Teaching, and others).

However, recently, because of diminishing job opportunities and the attraction of other sports careers, they have begun to look elsewhere. Some still see this as an attractive position because of the chance to work with young people and to teach them physical education skills. Often coaches come from the ranks of physical education teachers, so this too looms as one of the attractions of the profession.

State requirements vary regarding physical education but all mandate its inclusion in the curriculum. Pennsylvania states in its general curriculum regulations the following:

Each student in each grade shall participate in a planned program of physical education. The planned program shall include activities which:

1. Assist each student to attain and maintain a desirable level of physical fitness.
2. Develop desirable competencies for participation in sports lifetime in nature, team sports, and games.
3. Promote an understanding between regular physical activity and health.
4. Provide sports, games, and other physical activities that promote self-confidence and the ability to work in a group.
5. Require co-education instruction at the elementary, middle grade and/or junior high, and high school levels.

In recent years there has existed an increasing desire to educate young people to the importance of fitness, the joy of sports and athletics, and the value of lifetime sports. The President's Council on Physical Fitness and Sports defines physical fitness as the "ability to last, to bear up, to withstand stress, and to persevere under difficult circumstances where an unfit person would be ineffective or would quit."

Much the same as curriculum changes have occurred in other school subjects there has developed a "new fitness." It has taken several forms. Some of the most interesting have been The Play Factory at Emporia State University in Kansas and the New Games popular on the West Coast. These programs emphasize the fun aspects of sports. John O'Connell, codirector of the New Games Foundation, says that when they play they don't worry about who wins and who loses; they're concerned that people have fun. It's kind of a throwback to traditional play, community play, children's games, social recreation—to the time that people played together as a way to grow closer. Some persons who are not generally athletic or who have been inactive for years have been drawn to the new orientation. Several physical education teachers have organized such activities at their schools with success. The leisure revolution has resulted in a desire to expand participation in lifetime sports.

Some schools, often reflecting state requirements or guidelines, have made basic fundamental development their major emphasis. In addition, enrichment programs for talented students in PE have popped up around the country. These programs identify and encourage children to enhance their skills and interests. This might be a camping weekend (wall climbing, canoeing, fishing) or attendance at a college athletic contest. These new directions will continue to challenge and tax the energies and talents of physical education specialists.

DUTIES AND ACTIVITIES

Quite obviously, many demands and duties characterize the activities of the PE teacher. The following is a sampling.

The physical education specialist as a teacher engages in some of the following activities:

1. Determines the ability of students in their courses.
2. Revises instruction based upon students' abilities, that is, in teaching a skill (throwing a ball), aims it relative to what the class is able to do and proceeds from that point.
3. Prepares an equipment and materials-purchase budget and maintains it once obtained.
4. Utilizes an efficient system for reporting accidents and following them up.
5. Conducts special programs for children with physiological and psychological problems.
6. Provides information to the parents and community concerning the curriculum.
7. Promotes physical fitness in the school and community.
8. Helps students to commit themselves to self-improvement.
9. Prompts nonparticipating learners to join class activities and stay involved.

10. Develops a wide variety of skills in students, such as: accuracy, agility, balance, coordination, endurance, flexibility, power, rhythm, strength, timing, and other psychomotor abilities.

A TYPICAL DAY

The physical education instructor must maintain fitness not only as a model for students but to maintain the rigorous schedule that makes many demands upon the teacher. Consider a typical day in the life of a community/junior college PE instructor who serves as a basketball coach. Frances Garmon, presently at Delta State College in Mississippi, chose a home game day at her previous position at Temple Junior College in Texas:

5:30 a.m.	Alarm clock rings—arise.
6:30 a.m.	Depart for college.
6:33 a.m.	Stop at store for three area newspapers; check the accuracy of game time and location.
6:45 a.m.	Arrive at gym and office.
6:50 a.m.	Check dressing room to see if everything is in order for the game—warm-ups, uniforms, shoes, socks, and training supplies.
7:00 a.m.	Call all local radio stations to remind them once again about the game. Make a short tape over the phone for radio broadcast. Leave any game related information for the athletic office secretary.
7:45 a.m.	Review for class.
8:00–8:45 a.m.	Tennis class.
8:45 a.m.	Talk with and help students after class (special aid).
9:15 a.m.	Check to make sure the following are prepared for the game: officials, clock operator, 30-second clock operator, ticket sellers, ticket takers,

	scorekeeper, announcer, concessions, and business office. Also call to make arrangements to have game videotaped.
10:00 a.m.	Call the national office (NJCAA) and give them choices for top 20 rankings. Check mail. Call opponent to check if everything is okay and obtain arrival time of team.
11:00–11:50 a.m.	Swimming class.
12:00–1:00 p.m.	Lunch.
1:00–3:00 p.m.	Office work.
3:00–3:30 p.m.	Check out sound system, videotaping equipment, 30-second and game clock and all support personnel; have athletic secretary and cheerleaders call news media.
3:30–4:30 p.m.	Go home. Change and shower for game.
4:35 p.m.	Return to gym.
4:40 p.m.	Double-check dressing rooms, gym lights. Go over game strategy.
5:30 p.m.	Meet with Temple team, discuss game plan.
6:00 p.m.	Greet visiting team; manager shows them to locker room. Talk with coach to see if everything is okay; may need location of a restaurant for postgame meal.
6:30 p.m.	Taping and individual talks with Temple team. Stretching exercises in locker room.
7:00 p.m.	Team takes floor for warm-ups. Coaches report starting lineup.
7:15 p.m.	Return to dressing room.
7:25 p.m.	Return to court; player introductions.
7:30 p.m.	Game begins.
9:00 p.m.	Game concludes. Talk with team in the dressing room and then with the news media.

9:30 p.m.	Check on dressing rooms, have managers and cheerleaders call news media not present at the game.
9:35 p.m.	Prepare statistics.
10:30 p.m.	Stop on way home for a snack.
11:15 p.m.	Prepare for following day's classes; prepare practice schedules.
1:00 a.m.	Bedtime.

For those individuals who mesh teaching and coaching it's truly an unbelievable commitment. This combination requires intelligence, great energy and ability, and promises great rewards. If you wonder why they do it, Janet Lippincott, former PE teacher and coach at Springside School, has an answer. At the class level she enjoys teaching students the athletic skills of movement, efficiency, and balance, and then combining these general techniques with specific sports skills. When these students begin to play on a school team, I know they already have a good background in technical vocabulary and body mechanics and can concentrate on perfecting skills and various strategies. By teaching students at both levels she can see carryovers of their learning, reassess the class curriculum depending on their needs, and, best of all, watch their growth and development.

EDUCATION

Physical educators must obtain state certification as teachers. This takes place at a college that has an approved program for the education of PE teachers, such as the Rutgers University curriculum. Another (slightly different) program is that of Brigham Young University. Some areas exist for major emphasis within the teacher certification program: dance specialization; dance and sports; sports and teaching—elementary through secondary. In addition, students may also take a minor subject (an area in which some courses are taken; the number varies with the college) such as coaching, an academic area, or dance. Students may take a wide variety of practical and interesting courses. These are examples:

Jogging	Water safety instruction
Sports fundamentals:	Scuba diving, beginning
weight training	Children's dance methods
Advanced lifesaving	Sports officiating
Coaching team sports	Principles of physical
Softball	education
Karate, beginning	Fitness for living

In all programs for certification, in addition to professional physical education subjects, courses must be undertaken in the arts and sciences. At the University of Delaware these studies consist of four areas: communication skills, humanities, and fine arts; biological sciences; history and social sciences; and natural science and mathematics. Program requirements such as these attempt to provide the student with a cultural education appropriate for a college graduate.

A special experience characterizes the certification program called student teaching. This activity finds the college students, under the supervision of a cooperating teacher and a college faculty member, instructing school students. During this period of intensive training the future teacher practices and refines the skills necessary for a practicing professional. In sports medicine it would be called an internship or residency.

Most physical educators pursue graduate courses and master's degrees; a few will earn doctorates; some will obtain graduate degrees in physical education; others will undertake work in other areas. Florida State University offers special courses of study leading to Master of Science or Doctor of Philosophy degrees in motor learning and exercise physiology. The former has three areas of emphasis: motor learning, sport psychology, and motor development. The latter has subspecialties in anatomy, biomechanics, and exercise physiology. Florida State offers other programs in physical education at the master's and doctoral level, specifically designed for teachers and those wishing to enter administrative positions. For professional growth and financial reasons, PE teachers are urged to obtain a master's degree. For a faculty position at a community college this is a necessity. For those wishing to obtain a position as a PE department chairperson, advanced graduate work is required. Those seeking employment at the four-year college level will need to obtain a doctorate.

Job opportunities will remain only fair for PE teachers in the 1990s; however, salaries presently good will continue to improve. The recent upturn in the birth rate that has characterized the early 1980s will result in a growing need for additional teachers. Prospective physical educators are strongly urged to couple their major with courses in business, recreation, and/or communications. Joan Murtha, assistant in public relations for the North American Soccer League, graduated with a B.S. in physical education. However, she also took courses in recreation and business (marketing, accounting, and business law). Her summers were spent in teaching and coaching sports and in her free time she obtained valuable experience in sports-related activities. Murtha parlayed this into her present enjoyable position.

GETTING STARTED

If physical education instruction may become your career, visit with a PE teacher and discuss your plans. He or she will be able to suggest colleges as well as provide hints. In college, build into your program courses in communication arts and business to permit greater flexibility upon graduation. While teaching may be your first choice, career opportunities expand daily in sports and athletics and also exist as viable options. It is strongly suggested you obtain a student membership in your professional curriculum organization to help you stay current with your career and with potential job options. Write:

American Alliance for Physical Education, Health,
    Recreation and Dance
1900 Association Drive
Reston, VA 22091

The *Coaching Women's Basketball* magazine, because of its numerous articles on girls and women in athletics, should be reading for all PE people. Contact:

Coaching Women's Basketball
    P.O. Box 1170
    Cumming, GA 30130

CHAPTER 7

SPORTS MEDICINE

"If you're not good enough to play yet still want to be in on the sports action down on the field or on the court, seriously consider the position of athletic trainer."

Ronnie Barnes, M.S., ATC
Head Athletic Trainer
New York Giants Football Team

Perhaps the fastest-growing careers associated with sports have been those which fall into the category of sports medicine.

NEW ORIENTATION

The explosion of injuries at all levels and a desire by players, parents, and coaches to reduce them has created a greatly expanded need for sports medicine personnel. The growing concern with legal liability has also contributed to this movement. At the professional level, team owners, who pay players outstanding salaries, have hired people, purchased equipment, and established training programs to keep them healthy.

Historically, sports medicine personnel had been concerned with athletes only after an injury. Now strong emphasis has been placed upon injury avoidance. This takes place largely through conditioning. The new emphasis can be seen from The Athlete's Bill of Rights, below.

The Athlete's Bill of Rights

PROPER CONDITIONING helps to prevent injuries by hardening the body and increasing resistance to fatigue.

1. Are prospective players given directions and activities for preseason conditioning?
2. Is there a minimum of two weeks of practice before the first game or contest?
3. Is each player required to warm up thoroughly prior to participation?
4. Are substitutions made without hesitation when players evidence disability?

CAREFUL COACHING leads to skillful performance, which lowers the incidence of injuries.

1. Is emphasis given to safety in teaching techniques and elements of play?
2. Are injuries carefully analyzed to determine causes and suggest preventive programs?
3. Are tactics discouraged that may increase the hazards and thus the incidence of injuries?
4. Are practice periods carefully planned and of reasonable duration?

GOOD OFFICIATING promotes enjoyment of the game as well as the protection of players.

1. Are players as well as coaches thoroughly schooled in the rules of the games?
2. Are rules and regulations strictly enforced in practice periods as well as in games?
3. Are officials employed who are qualified both emotionally and technically for their responsibilities?

RIGHT EQUIPMENT AND FACILITIES serve a unique purpose in protection of players.

1. Is the best protective equipment provided for contact sports?

2. Is careful attention given to proper fitting and adjustment of equipment?
3. Is equipment properly maintained, and are worn and outmoded items discarded?
4. Are proper areas for play provided and carefully maintained?

ADEQUATE MEDICAL CARE is a necessity in the prevention and control of athletic injuries.

1. Is there a thorough preseason health history and medical examination?
2. Is a physician present at contests and readily available during practice sessions?
3. Does the physician make the decision as to whether an athlete should return to play following injury during games?
4. Is authority from a physician required before an athlete can return to practice after being out of play because of disabling injury?
5. Is the care given athletes by coach or trainer limited to first aid and medically prescribed services?

The importance of proper conditioning involving strength, cardiovascular fitness, and flexibility cannot be overemphasized. Listed below are the Ten Cardinal Principles of Athletic Conditioning that every coach, player, and sports medicine professional must know and implement.

1. Warm up—each activity must be preceded by an adequate warmup. Following this step, stretching activities and running will provide the greatest benefit. Warming down likewise requires attention.
2. Gradualness—start slowly to condition someone and look to peak at a certain time. Setting goals can be helpful.
3. Timing—Athletes must be counseled not to overdo workouts; relaxation and rest form part of every conditioning program.
4. Intensity—workouts and practices must be characterized by quality and continuous activity with appropriate rest periods.

5. Capacity level—while cautious to avoid the above pitfalls, athletes will want to work to capacity and should have the encouragement to do so.
6. Strength—greater endurance, speed, flexibility, and confidence will result from improved strength. This will also decrease vulnerability to injury.
7. Motivation—sports medicine personnel can reinforce the coaches' techniques to stimulate players.
8. Specialization—include in each player's conditioning program exercises to improve the player in relation to the sport he or she wishes to play and her or his weakness.
9. Relaxation—trainers should familiarize themselves with specific techniques to teach players how to relax and thereby recover from tension, fatigue, and stress.
10. Routine—a planned daily, weekly, and monthly routine must be constructed for each player in cooperation with the athlete and coach.

The above principles should serve as guidelines. Careful adherence can make an important difference to athletes. For example, in the area of warming up, one study at Duke University conducted by lacrosse coach Waldman found over 50 percent of injuries occur in the first quarter! In addition, the author has further observed that many injuries occur in the beginning of practice. Consequently, it's a must for players to warm up even if they are late, and practice has already begun.

An examination of the careers related to sports medicine follows.

ATHLETIC TRAINERS

An athletic trainer's duties consist of the implementation of an injury prevention program, and the initiation of immediate treatment and rehabilitation procedures for the injured athlete as directed by the team physician. He or she is the person you see down on the field or sitting on the bench close to the large first aid kit. Long before the contest, the trainer has prepared the participants, taping some and providing therapy for others. He or she will stay after the game, providing services as needed.

Specifically, trainers engage in the following activities:

1. Designing and monitoring a program of conditioning in cooperation with the coaching staff.
2. Supervision of safety factors involving playing areas.
3. Selection of proper equipment in cooperation with the coaching staff and equipment manager (see below).
4. Administration of first aid to injured athletes.
5. Application of devices such as braces and bandages to prevent injury.
6. Development and supervision of the rehabilitation program for an injured athlete under the supervision of a physician. This may involve the use of whirlpool or ultrasound equipment. Often the trainer will show the athlete exercises to do to prevent a recurring injury and then monitor the improvement of muscle strength.
7. Maintenance of the athletic training area and performance of such tasks as ordering supplies, supervising the servicing of equipment, and keeping careful records.
8. Development of good working relationships with the players, coaches, physicians, and with the school authorities or professional management.

Quite obviously the duties and obligations are quite significant and the athletic trainer's importance to sports continues to increase. Otho Davis, head trainer for the Philadelphia Eagles and executive director of the National Athletic Trainers Association, believes that the most important role of the trainer is to prevent an injury from occurring, because at the professional level a player cannot afford to miss practice. For the Eagles, conditioning occurs 11 months a year! After a month break following the season many players begin a new program. On two days, running for cardiovascular endurance and agility is emphasized along with three days of weight training. A sense of the commitment of some of the team can be gained from former Eagle and present Rowan College (NJ) football coach John Bunting, who spent an average of six hours a day rehabilitating his knee following an operation. Trainer Davis believes that his greatest satisfaction comes from seeing an athlete return to maximum potential by performing well after an injury.

Another area of recent concern is that of injury prevention as related to equipment selection. The trainer works as a member of a team composed of the coach and equipment manager and is guided by the following in choosing equipment:

1. Its specifications must provide maximum protection for the area to be protected.
2. It must be able to withstand repeated use with no decrease in efficiency.
3. It must fit carefully so that it can provide protection under playing conditions.
4. It must not impede the player's activity (as nearly as possible).
5. It must not create a hazard to other contestants. States and leagues usually have a rule against this.
6. It must be replaced when it is no longer effective and has lost its protective value.

Athletic training offers a demanding and an enjoyable career for persons interested in athletics. The working conditions and salary vary greatly. At the school level, most teach courses and serve as trainers part time, for which they receive additional compensation similar to coaches, on the average $40,000 a year. College trainers work full time in this capacity and enjoy greater prestige than their high school counterparts but have similar salaries. Those who teach and serve as trainers at the university level earn considerably more. Professional trainers' salaries vary with the team; some work part time only when the sport is in season, others work year-round and receive good salaries. Ronnie Barnes, head athletic trainer, N.Y. Giants football team, believes salaries have not accelerated because many people like their jobs so much they're willing to accept lesser salaries. Ronnie believes salaries will improve considerably in the second half of the 90s.

EDUCATION

Once you believe you have the physical and psychological qualities to become an athletic trainer, begin by taking science-related courses in high school (health, chemistry, etc.). Talk with your school counselor concerning your interest and obtain information about colleges with programs approved by the National Athletic Trainers Association (see address below). In college you will take both liberal arts (English, history, science) and professional education subjects. The latter courses at the University of Delaware are typical of those taken in programs to prepare athletic trainers:

Anatomy and physiology	First aid/athletic injuries
Human growth and develop-	Advanced First Aid/athletic
ment	injuries
Psychology and techniques	Biomechanics
of coaching	Practicum in athletic
Human anatomy	training

In addition to completing the courses for graduation, a significant number of hours of practical work and an examination must be passed for NATA certification as an athletic trainer. Persons may obtain approval in other ways: the apprenticeship program (for persons graduating from colleges not offering athletic training); graduation from a physical therapy program; and through special arrangements for trainers with experience.

Many opportunities for positions in athletic training will exist in the years ahead.

SPORTS PHYSICIAN

At the center of the sports medicine profession are the sports medicine physicians—orthopedists, osteopaths, and chiropractors. Regardless of the specialty of the physician, the commandments of Theodore Fox, M.D., formerly of the Chicago Bears professional football team, deserve serious attention as guidelines to behavior. These have undergone slight modification to conform to this book.

TEAM OR SPORTS PHYSICIAN'S
TEN COMMANDMENTS

1. The physician must be trained in all procedures for prevention, recognition, diagnosis, and treatment of injuries, first aid as well as knowledge of soft tissue and skeletal injuries.
2. The physician must personally examine and evaluate all candidates for the sport or team *prior* to their participation to determine each individual's fitness for the same.

   This should include a history on all previous illnesses, accidents, and surgical procedures as well as a psychological evaluation and a thorough physical examination.

   The physical evaluation should include observations of any physical characteristics and defects predisposing the player to injury, especially in the collision sports. The physical examination should include determination of the individual's maturity, balance, coordination, agility, stamina, and strength.
3. The physician must know the basic fundamentals of the particular sport with which he or she is involved, to better understand the mechanism of the injuries occurring, as well as the injured participant and her or his problem.
4. The physician must observe and evaluate the emotional well-being of the athlete, especially the young player. Is the candidate being pushed by a frustrated parent to be a superstar or made apprehensive by a parent because he or she might get hurt?

5. The physician should *fit* and select all protective gear and equipment and check it as to type and quality, especially in the collision sports.

6. The physician should supervise the trainer or the coach in the proper use of physiotherapeutic techniques used in the training room. Also, the physician is responsible for conditioning and rehabilitation exercises (such as weight training).

   Upon the doctor rests the responsibility for total rehabilitation of the injured athlete (mental and physical); a careful examination must precede returning to participation.

7. The physician must advise the coach not to teach dangerous blocking and checking practices and the avoidance of mismatches between athletes, especially young players.

   The doctor should advise the coach or trainer about problems or injuries that may occur because of heat, humidity, overwork, or fatigue.

8. The physician (or a designated replacement) must be available at all times to examine the injured player *as soon as possible* after the injury. This is especially true in collision sports where, if possible, the physician should be on the field.

   Often youngsters will mask an injury so as to continue to play; a physician can make an assessment of the severity of the injury. Also, certain injuries (neck, reinjury) require a doctor's examination.

9. The physician must prevent an injured player from returning to the game if there exists a reasonable doubt about the player's condition. In doing so the physician must resist all pressures from coaches, parents, alumni, and the player.

10. The doctor must obtain X rays of injuries (and other information as necessary) prior to judging the condition of the injury.

The importance of the physician to sports may not be realized by the average fan, but the athlete realizes the contribution. Gale Sayers, Hall of Fame running back at Kansas and with the Chicago Bears, gives his opinion in his fine book, *I Am Third* (Bantam):

> The business of injuries to professional football players is a tricky one, with all kinds of complications. You really have to leave it up to the team doctor. I have always found Dr. Fox a man I could rely on, a man I could go to if I had problems. My philosophy about aches and pains is to get them checked out to be sure they're not going to impair your performance.

Dave Meggyesy, also a former professional football player, echoes the significant role physicians play, recalling some negative experiences in college (*Out of Their League;* Ramparts):

> When a player is injured, he is sent to the team physician who is usually more concerned with getting the athlete back into action than anything else. This reversal of priorities leads to unbelievable abuses.

The sports medicine staff has a serious obligation to the player's *present and future health.* Close adherence to Dr. Fox's Ten Commandments will curtail many of the serious abuses related to athletics.

ORTHOPEDIST

While some teams employ general practitioners (GPs) in the capacity of sports physicians, orthopedists by their training best serve in this position. Orthopedists are medical doctors (MDs) who treat injuries to the skeletal system—backs, necks, arms, legs and joints, and to the body's muscles. Those involved in sports normally serve on a consulting basis with teams and/or work in sports clinics.

They are the geniuses and miracle doctors who frequently save careers and lead in developing new surgical procedures. Consequently, this career is the best paid of all sports medicine personnel. Yearly salaries over $250,000 are common. In addition, they enjoy fine working conditions and, in most cases, great prestige. These doctors attend undergraduate college and then enter medical school. After graduation, they concentrate on their chosen field. This involves more course work, individual study, and a practical experience. The internship takes one year and the residency normally four years, so the total education of the orthopedist takes nine years after college! During residency period, the young doctor works under the supervision of an experienced orthopedic physician, conducting examinations, directing first aid, performing surgery, and designing rehabilitation programs. Not all orthopedists go into sports medicine; some set up private practice and work to correct deformities related mainly to muscle, joint, and bone problems. If a person has a serious accident requiring surgery such as cartilage damage to a knee or a hip replacement, an orthopedist would be involved. With increased attention to injury prevention and rehabilitation, opportunities for careers as a doctor with a specialty in orthopedics will continue to be very good.

OSTEOPATH

Osteopathic physicians (DOs) concentrate on the muscularskeletal system of the body in returning the injured athlete to action. As do medical doctors (MDs), they utilize surgery, drugs, and other acceptable health care practices. In addition, they may use manipulation and emphasize the treatment of the whole athlete in designing a conditioning or rehabilitation program.

While still not totally accepted by medical doctors, osteopathic medicine has made great gains in recent years. In Detroit all four professional sports teams utilize DOs as their team physicians. The educational requirements of osteopathic college almost parallel those of medical colleges and DOs wishing to specialize likewise complete a rigorous residency.

Salaries of doctors of osteopathy lag behind those of medical doctors. However, most do well—$75,000–$100,000 a year—and those in sports medicine do even better. Opportunities for employment for osteopaths in the future will continue to remain very good as sports medicine expands and the public comes to further respect the work of doctors of osteopathic medicine.

CHIROPRACTOR

Stewart Himmelstein participated in athletics in high school (football, baseball, martial arts). Following an injury, "I went to a chiropractor and became interested in the field. The doctor talked about prevention of injury and increasing optimal health; I liked that. I became more sensitive to the way I slept, the way I rode in my car, and the way I conducted myself physically."

Himmelstein attends New York Chiropractic College in Seneca Falls, N.Y. Following graduation and receipt of his Doctor of Chiropractic degree, he plans to specialize and become certified in sports medicine which means additional study, exams, and close work with a sports medicine physician. "I like chiropractic because as an athlete you have to balance yourself physically, mentally, and chemically—this is what chiropractic does." Himmelstein suggests those considering the field become proficient in communication skills. You deal with people and groups all the time, so study science and visit and talk with a chiropractor who works with athletes.

As with osteopaths a small percent of chiropractors serve in a consulting capacity to sports teams. Doctors of Chiropractic emphasize the utilization of manipulation (adjustments) as their primary treatment. They do not believe in using prescription drugs or surgery nor are they permitted to do so by state law. Chiropractors do employ other treatments with the injured athlete—heat, water, diet, nutritional supplementation, massage therapy, and others.

Chiropractic colleges require two years of college as a condition of enrollment. At these colleges students pursue courses in the biological sciences and in chiropractic principles and also undertake a clinical experience. Most chiropractors engage in a private office practice earning salaries in the $40,000-a-year range; those with an emphasis in sports will earn more. The growing interest in holistic medicine and the unique contribution of chiropractic to sports medicine will insure growing opportunities for interested individuals.

SUMMARY—SPORTS PHYSICIANS

Individuals considering a career as a sports physician should realize the academic commitment necessary. Excellent grades and an interest and competence in science remain a must.

If you're planning a career in this area, a long commitment to academics is necessary. In addition, these specialties require passing a licensure examination to practice medicine in the state of your choice.

Sports physicians have a strong interest in improving their profession; many conduct research on various aspects of athletic performance. In addition these individuals work well with people and have a strong interest in athletics and sports. These readings are suggested:

Helping Hands: Challenge of Medicine
Helping Hands: Financing a Health Career
    Order Department
    American Medical Association
    (see address on next page)

Medicine—A Woman's Career
    American Medical Women's Association
    740 Broadway
    New York, NY 10019

Health Care for the Female Athlete
    The Athletics Institute
    200 North Castlewood Drive
    North Palm Beach, FL 33408

Opportunities in Health and Medical Careers
VGM Career Horizons

Opportunities in Chiropractic Health Care
VGM Career Horizons

Opportunities in Physician Careers
VGM Career Horizons

The following organizations provide additional information:

American Medical Association
535 North Dearborn Street
Chicago, IL 60610

Association of American Medical Colleges
One DuPont Circle N.W., Suite 200
Washington, DC 20036

American Osteopathic Association
212 East Ohio Street
Chicago, IL 60611

American Chiropractic Association
2220 Grand Avenue
Des Moines, IA 50312

PHYSICAL THERAPY

The field of sports physical therapy exploded during the 1980s and now in the 1990s it shows no signs of slowing. Testimony to this growth has been the dramatic increase in applications to colleges offering physical therapy programs and the expansion of physical therapy centers. Pat Croce, L.P.T., ATC's Sports Physical Therapists, Inc. headquartered in Bryn Mawr, Pennsylvania, has grown from a one-clinic operation to several centers in several states. They serve not only school, college, and professional athletes along with weekend athletes, but also others who wish to avail themselves of the aggressive innovative techniques of sports physical therapy to return to maximum health as soon as possible.

Physical therapists work with athletes who have been disabled through accident, birth defect, or illness. Some therapists work with athletes sent to them by a physician, to aid in the rehabilitation of an injury. Treatments include (1) exercises for increasing strength, endurance, coordination, and range of motion; (2) activities to facilitate motor capacity or learning; (3) instruction in activities of daily living and use of assistance devices; and (4) application of physical agents such as heat and cold, sound, water, and acupuncture to relieve pain and/or alter physiological status.

Physical therapists attend college to receive certification in their profession; some attend graduate programs and enter leadership positions in the field. Certification requires pursuing certain course work and in 49 of 50 states passing an examination to receive a license to treat patients.

Many physical therapists who work with athletes do so at sports medicine clinics where they assist other professionals in rehabilitating athletes. This team approach will undoubtedly characterize medicine for the future. Jim Corea, Ph.D., R.P.T., is one physical therapist who works with both athletes and the general public. At his center (Moorestown, NJ) he consults and works with many athletes and coaches, making suggestions and writing publications on weight training, conditioning, and nutrition. In addition, he hosts a nightly radio talk show offering guidance in the area of health and nutrition on WWDB-FM in Philadelphia.

Salaries, presently in the $45,000 to $60,000 range, will continue to grow as the sports profession and the public continue to realize the value of physical therapy.

PARAPROFESSIONALS

Two paraprofessionals aid the patient—the *physical therapist assistant* and the *physical therapy aide*. The former graduates from a two-year program with a major in physical therapy; the latter learns on the job. Each of these works under the supervision of a professional physical therapist who in turn works under supervision of a physician. Salaries for assistants range in the $18,000 to $30,000 category while those for aides average $18,000. These exist as viable options for those not wanting four years (or more) of college.

If you wish additional information about these specialties, contact:

American Physical Therapy Association
1111 North Fairfax Street
Alexandria, VA 22314

and read *Opportunities in Physical Therapy Careers* and *Opportunities in Paramedical Careers,* VGM Career Horizons series.

A periodical with valuable information for those considering entering the PT field is *Rehab Management;* it contains articles such as "Sports Injury Management" and "Taking a Proactive Approach to Sports Medicine Injuries." It may be purchased from:

Rehab Management
1849 Sawtelle Boulevard, Suite 770
Los Angeles, CA 90025

OTHER SPORTS MEDICINE OPPORTUNITIES

The fabulous growth of sports medicine has touched every area of the medical and allied medical professions. *Dentists, podiatrists, othotists* and *prosthetists, optometrists* and *ophthalmologists,* and *nutritionists* have applied their unique skills and knowledge to improve athletic performance. For example, dentists are working on a special mouthpiece believed to improve strength and reduce fatigue for some athletes.

Podiatrists prepare special inserts for shoes for injured athletes or those with chronic problems. Orthotists and prosthetists assist injured athletes with special equipment to return them to action and prevent reinjury. Optometrists and ophthalmologists, vision specialists, properly evaluate and fit athletes with corrective glasses. Some have had excellent success with vision exercises for improving athletic performance. The explosion of research linking diet and supplementation (using vitamins and minerals) and sports success has placed nutritionists in the forefront of the movement to reduce injuries and increase athletic performance. Additional information about these and other sports medicine careers may be found in the VGM Career Horizons book *Opportunities in Sports Medicine Careers.* The *Sports Medicine Book,* by Gabe Merkin, M.D. and Marshall Hoffman, while somewhat traditional, provides much useful information for the athlete and the aspiring sports medicine professional.

SPORTS MEDICINE CLINICS AND CENTERS

In recent years there has been an expanded interest in the team approach to the prevention and treatment of athletic injuries. The previous information on the athletic trainers, sports physicians, and physical therapists emphasized the importance of these individuals working together. In accordance with this team concept, there is a strong trend toward injured athletes being treated at sports medicine clinics or centers. Most often these exist in one of three settings: at universities related to medical schools, at hospitals, and as private enterprises in medical buildings. The former serves the college community, particularly the athletes as well as outsiders; frequently the center conducts research on new methods of conditioning and injury rehabilitation and often offers sports medicine clinics for coaches and others. Typical is the fine Temple University Center for Sports Medicine and Science. The center employs on a full-time basis orthopedic surgeons, certified athletic trainers, physical therapists, and a supportive clerical staff. In addition, the following part-timers lend their talents—a sports podiatrist, a cardiologist, an exercise physiologist, a nutritionist, a technician for stress testing, and two orthopedic surgeons. In special cases, other health professionals will provide consultation. For example, in the case of a broken nose, a doctor specializing in ear, nose, and throat will be involved. Ted Quendenfeld, administrative director for the center, says that 90 percent of their cases come from outside referral. But this is only one part of the program, which has also an educational and research component. In fact, as part of the center's educational commitment, Quendenfeld, an athletic trainer, gives over 100 presentations a year to coaches, athletes, and trainers.

As sports medicine clinics and centers expand, they will be an important source of employment for athletic trainers, physical therapists, and physicians. They offer more flexibility in terms of activities than traditionally found in these careers.

Sports medicine professionals make an important contribution to athletics; all sports enthusiasts deserve to give these occupations serious consideration when choosing a career. In addition, Dr. Ron Feingold, sports medicine specialist at Adelphi University in Garden City, New York, maintains that the job market is unlimited—now and in the future.

GETTING STARTED

If you are a student, while in high school or college you can gain valuable experience by serving as a student athletic trainer. Such a person normally performs the following tasks:

1. Helps maintain the training room and the supplies.
2. Aids with the taping and treatments.
3. Prepares field kits and has them available during contests and practices.
4. Reports new injuries to coach and trainer.
5. Prepares a beverage and has it ready for athletes' breaks during games and practices.
6. Completes a course for student trainers.

7. Keeps student trainer duties separate from student manager responsibilities.
8. Aids in record keeping of player injuries and treatment.
9. Performs related tasks as asked by coach, trainer, or physician.
10. Maintains a professional rapport with players, coaches, physician, trainer, and with opposing team and its personnel.

Many colleges and high schools utilize female student athletic trainers. Excellent career opportunities exist for women athletic trainers. Holly Wilson, former athletic trainer at Indiana State, recently wrote that though women's entrance into the field had been slow, it's now beginning to gain momentum because of the rapid growth of interscholastic and intercollegiate athletic programs for girls and women. In fact, women may come to dominate the field through sheer numbers. If the profession interests you and you are a student, actively pursue the following:

1. Join the NATA as a student member and request career education information:

   National Athletic Trainers Association
   2952 Stemmons Freeway
   Suite 200
   Dallas, TX 75247–6103

2. Obtain a position as a student trainer.
3. Choose your courses carefully to prepare you for your career and do well in school and college.
4. Read about your future careers; read the materials suggested in this chapter and at the end of the book in Appendix D.
5. Attend a program for student athletic trainers.

   Cramer, a company which produces athletic training materials, sponsors several trainers' workshops and can provide related materials. Write:

Cramer Products
   P.O. Box 1001
   Gardner, KS 66030

6. Regularly read the *First Aider* Newsletter (Cramer Products) and the *Sports Medicine Guide,* a regularly published newsletter available from:

Mueller Sports Medicine
   One Quench Drive
   Prairie du Sac, WI 53578

7. Contact the Gatorade Sports Science Institute; it offers a number of publications (free) on sports nutrition, sports injuries, conditioning and training, and other related topics. The address for the *Sports Science Exchange* publications follows:

Gatorade Sports Science Institute
   SSE Subscription Offer
   % Quaker Oats Co.
   P.O. Box 049001
   Chicago, IL 60604–9001

8. Consider subscribing to the *Merkin Report,* a newsletter on fitness, nutrition, and health.

The *Merkin Report*
   Box 6608
   Silver Spring, MD 20916

The strong desire from all segments of society and the sports world to curtail athletic injuries will ensure varied, interesting, and profitable career opportunities in sports medicine in the future.

CHAPTER 8

PUBLIC RELATIONS

He works with Michael Jordan, David Robinson, Theresa Edwards, Chris Mullen, Karl Malone, Coach Chuck Daly, Coach Teresa Grentz, and television and radio personalities worldwide!

Who is he? Craig Miller, the assistant executive director for public relations for the U.S.A. Basketball and the 1992 Olympic team. It all started when he was a college student.

Craig attended Albion College in Michigan where he was a starting offensive lineman in football, an all-star in lacrosse, and a good student. However, his interest in sports did not stop here. During his college years he served as: sports editor, college yearbook; sports director, radio station; sports editor, college newspaper; and student sports intramural director. This fine background catapulted him into the position of sports editor of the *Milford Times* newspaper. At the paper he gained excellent experience writing, editing, and laying out the sports section.

These valuable experiences landed him the position of sports information director at Earlham College in Indiana and then a similar position at Villanova University. In addition, he has enjoyed a number of wonderful short-term assignments such as game program editor for the McDonald's All American High School Game, Game Day public relations assistant for the Philadelphia Eagles and Philadelphia 76ers, and 1988 U.S. Olympic Committee press officer for men and women's track and field. Craig paid his dues and has enjoyed every minute.

"Those interested in sports public relations will have a bright future. Computer knowledge and experience with desktop publishing are important," states Miller. "Even more important is writing experience and becoming involved (radio, student newspaper, etc.). You must be capable of producing features as well as press releases."

Craig further reminds potential public relation specialists, "There are long hours and constant seven-day work weeks—I know on the college level I worked seven days a week from August until May!"

The public's hunger for information about their team, favorite player, the next opponent must be satisfied. Those desires are met through the efforts of public relations personnel.

One of the most popular academic areas on campuses today is that of communications major. Within that broad subject field, one of the most exciting specialties involves sports.

The expansion of public relations extends to schools, colleges, sports organizations, and professional teams. PR people work to maintain a favorable opinion of their institutions. Those in sports work to obtain publicity to fill stadiums, increase the visibility of colleges, and promote players. The activities vary with the size of the college. For professional teams, the PR program will vary with the team level; major-league team agents will be busier than those at the lower levels. Another major factor that will affect this office's work is the success of the team and its players. Successful teams create great interest and consequently test the energies of the PR staff.

PROFESSIONAL TEAMS

Lenny Moore, who served as outstanding running back on the Baltimore Colts professional football team, until recently worked in a public relations capacity for the team. This is his demanding schedule:

8:15 a.m.   Arrive at the office forty-five minutes early to prepare for the day before the telephones start ringing.

9:00 a.m.	Representative activities
	a. Set up schedule of appearances to be made by the players and himself.
	b. Send out correspondence to persons requesting appearances and other information.
	c. Attend meeting in reference to co-chairing a charitable event (Heart Fund, Sickle Cell Anemia, MS, Leukemia).
	d. Coordinate with Assistant General Manager on update of programs, potential problems, or general information sharing.
7:30 p.m.	Attend a sports affair; make a presentation and show film of team highlights during the previous season.

Some weeks he works seven days and nights! He works with senior citizens' organizations, jails, schools, community recreation programs, business and civic groups, hospitals, and others.

Professional teams work closely with the news media on a daily basis, providing them a wide variety of information. Often following a major trade, a firing, or the signing of a number one draft choice, PR people go into high gear as public interest reaches a frenzy. However, even the daily schedules are hectic.

Chick McElrone serves as Assistant Director of Public Relations for the Philadelphia Eagles and follows the schedule below on a typical Monday during the season:

8:45 a.m.	Arrive at office. Check morning newspaper for previous day's game stories and quotes from players and coaches for possible inclusion in weekly news release.
9:00 a.m.	Begin preparation of weekly news release to include review of previous day's game highlights and key information of upcoming week's

	game. Also include alphabetical and numerical rosters, depth charts, and updated season statistics, both team and individuals. Call team medical personnel to include information in the release and project playing availability of players injured in previous day's game.
10:30 a.m.	Check room where coach's weekly press conference will be held at 11:30 a.m. Make sure room is clean, tables and chairs are in order, public address system is working properly, and (when involved) caterer is prepared to feed lunch to the anticipated number of news media personnel expected to attend.
11:20 a.m.	Pass out news releases, statistical and injury information prior to coach's arrival for press conference.
11:30 a.m.	Tape record press conference for late arriving members of the media or for later playback for those who could not attend because of distance or some extenuating circumstance.
12:30 p.m.	Dine with news media.
1:00 p.m.	Return to office to catch up on phone messages and special requests which may have come in during the press conference.
3:00 p.m.	Accompany news media to practice field and locker room to be available to answer any questions or provide assistance.
4:00 p.m.	Visit or call local printer for last-minute changes in upcoming game program magazine. If the next game will be played away, compile material you will need for game advance publicity work; for example, player and coaching staff

	pictures, TV film clips, newspaper clips, news releases, rosters, statistics, and your own club's news media guides.
5:00 p.m.	Call key members of news media in city whose team you will be playing next. If they will be traveling to your city, ask if they have any special needs or requests that you might fill. If you will be traveling in advance of any away game to their city, ask them if there is anything special that you might bring with you to help them write about your team. Check with the other team's writers about setting up phone interviews with personnel from your team later in the week.
6:30 p.m.	Leave office.

In most cases sports publicity people for professional teams come from sports staffs of newspapers or from college campuses where they served as sports information directors. These individuals know how to work with the media and the public they serve.

COLLEGE POSITIONS

At the college level the public relations specialist for athletics is called *Sports Information Director* (SID). Don Kopriva, SID, University of Wisconsin, Parkside, and former Secretary of the College Sports Information Directors of America (CoSIDA), said that a typical sports information staff varies from school to school, depending upon enrollment, budget, and other factors. Many large colleges have three professionals, a few secretaries, and many student assistants; many small schools may have only a part-time SID (or none at all).

Here are some of the typical activities of sports publicists at the college and professional levels:

Establish excellent interpersonal relationships—with athletic and school administrators, with coaching staff and players, and with the print and electronic journalists.

Prepare press guide—a booklet containing information on each player and the team that frequently contains statistics and records for the sport. At the professional level a team yearbook is produced.

Organize press briefings—arrange for and meet with newspaper writers and TV and radio reporters to bring them information about a player or a team.

Arrange press conferences—coordinate meetings with the press for the coach and/or players.

Send news releases to media—usually a couple of pages of typing that provides new information to the newspapers, radio, and TV.

Send specific news releases—these provide information to a player's hometown newspaper, for example.

Maintain files—collect information on athletes and teams (historical and statistical data).

Direct press box— for certain sports, arrange for seating and materials for newspaper, radio, and television people, as well as for distribution of admission credentials.

Maintain scrapbook—clip newspaper items about the team(s) and players.

Arrange for photography—photographs of each player (head and shoulders) must be taken and action team photos and film (color for TV). Films and photographs are made available to the media.

Answer requests—information to the league office, other teams, and to the general public.

Write stories—not all newspapers can send a reporter to cover an event, so a story often is written by the sports publicist and distributed.

Engage in professional development and growth—through conferences, meetings, and readings concerning innovations and changes (cable television, endorsements, NCAA and NAIA regulations, etc.)

GETTING STARTED

Prepare for this career by taking high school courses in writing, computers, television, public speaking, journalism, and photography. A few opportunities exist for high school graduates who show very special ability or expertise (photography, video). However, attending college and majoring in communications with an emphasis in journalism and/or radio-TV with electives in public relations and physical education will provide an excellent background. Also, if available, take an elective in sport studies—a course such as Sports and Society or The History of Sports. These will prove valuable.

Try to obtain a position as a part-time student aide in the Sports Information Office; if that is not possible, valuable alternatives are student newspaper work, playing a sport, or working for the college radio station, newspaper, yearbook, or television station.

Average salaries are good ($40,000–$80,000), but beginning salaries lag behind those of other college graduates. Of course, if you enjoy sports, the working conditions are excellent. Two books worth reading, *Opportunities in Public Relations* and *Opportunities in Journalism* (both VGM Career Horizons), will provide additional insights into this career.

If you think you want to work at the college level, join:

The College Sports Information
    Directors of America
    Fred Nuesch, Secretary
    Campus Box 114
    Texas A & I University
    Kingsville, TX 78363

CHAPTER 9

ADDITIONAL SPORTS CAREERS

Sports attract not only athletes and fans but a great range of individuals who have managed to link their work and athletics to the improvement of both.

SPORTS EQUIPMENT SALES AND DEVELOPMENT

The expansion of interest in sports has resulted in an explosion of sports products, including sports equipment, sportswear, and sports novelties.

People develop, design, produce, and market these items. The fitness craze has resulted in equipment (stairmaster, cross-country skiing simulator, etc.) unknown a decade ago; shoes exist for every conceivable type of athletic activity; and fads in sportswear change monthly.

Annually the National Sporting Goods Association hosts an expo in Chicago—thousands of products greet the participant. Some come to find new products for a sports equipment/clothing store they own, others look for a hot item to market to teams, and a few come to get clues about a product that they hope to develop and market.

If you enjoy sales, sporting goods sales may constitute a career option for you. Wendy Heffernan, sales associate for Foot Locker, said, "In high school I went for a job in an industry I knew I would like—I've been here since, through high school and college. Anyone who's interested in sports would benefit from this job." Heffernen serves as a high school girls basketball coach. "As a coach it's a great advantage to see new products arriving on the scene and obtaining feedback on their performance from customers."

The National Sporting Goods Association
1699 Wall Street
Mt. Prospect, IL 60056–5780

SPORTS PSYCHOLOGIST

"I can work with troubled athletes (chemical dependency, emotional problems, etc.) but I like to think of myself as an educator rather than a therapist," said Dr. Joan Ingalls. Many sports psychologists utilize techniques such as visual training and mental practice to enhance performance of athletes. Ingalls provides such services at her New York City practice, but also teaches part-time at William Patterson College.

Sports psychologists function in a number of ways—as consultants to teams and clinics, as college professors, and as private office practitioners. However, some of those acting as sports psychologists have had no training in psychology! Many other persons have backgrounds in physical education, athletic training, and exercise physiology. Dr. William Morgan, University of Wisconsin, believes that this is harmful and that only those with training degrees (M.A., Ph.D.) in psychology should function as sports psychologists. Only those trained as psychologists can obtain malpractice insurance.

As more individuals educated in psychology become available, they will replace those with inadequate backgrounds. Consequently, this field has ample career opportunities.

Sports psychology requires two years (M.A.) to four years (Ph.D.) training beyond four years of college. Excellent grades are a must. Most pursuing this major will try to mesh it with some electives in sports studies and/or athletic training to increase their understanding of the sports world. Salaries average from $30,000–100,000; those in private practice with consulting positions with teams do best. For additional information, contact:

The Journal of Sports Psychology
Human Kinetics Publishers
P.O. Box 5076
Champaign, IL 61820

The Academy for the Psychology of Sports
International
2062 Arlington Avenue
Toledo, OH 43609

Sports Psychology Program
University of North Carolina at Greensboro
Greensboro, NC 27412
(Request a pamphlet entitled *Sports Psychology and Counseling.*)

SPORTS PHOTOGRAPHER—STILL AND MOTION

Want to be close to the sports excitement? Want to be down on the field for an athletic event?

Consider photographing the event.

Sports photographers capture on film some of the beauty of sports. A good sports photographer possesses excellent skills developed through many years of experience. If this sounds too demanding, consider beginning your career by "shooting" an amateur competition with a small instamatic photographic camera or an inexpensive cartridge motion picture or video camera. If your interest develops, purchase more sophisticated equipment. Many local newspapers and school yearbooks need photographs; ask them if they would like some of yours. You may even be paid! Many schools film and videotape athletic events for students, players, and coaches to review. This may be an opportunity to gain some experience while aiding the school.

Jerry Gay, an award-winning sports photographer, traces his love of his profession to his youth. In junior high school, he dreamed of someday becoming a big football star, but his dentist advised him to avoid all contact with sports while he was wearing braces. So he became a photographer. He believes that becoming a successful photographer is like becoming a successful athlete; it takes a lot of hard work and patience to make the major leagues. But when you get there, you're glad you paid your dues.

Some photographers work for specific magazines or newspapers. If these are general publications, the photography staff will cover subjects other than sports; while a few photographers may specialize in athletics, they well may be called upon to work on other assignments. Naturally, those employed by sports magazines or newspapers would only work in athletics.

A significant number of photographers in this field work as freelancers. This means they are self-employed and work for a number of publications. Some will receive specific assignments to cover particular events and will sell the "shots" they take. Others will work part-time for a couple of newspapers, supplying them with several photographs a week. Still others may attend games and hope they will get some photos of a spectacular event to sell to a magazine or newspaper.

Many film and video people function in the same capacity, although many full-time positions exist. After working for a number of video organizations Mike DiTrolio began his own business, Sports Photography—Video Network (SPVN), located in Springfield, PA. In this capacity he develops season highlight films for college teams (a twenty-minute summary of the team's successes). He is responsible for the taping, editing, and final production. Alumni, potential recruits, and community organizations see and enjoy these videos. In the area of photography DiTrolio takes individual and team photographs of school, community, and club teams. When not totally absorbed in sports he occasionally will videotape religious and corporate events and festivities and do a school or college highlight video. "I love what I do because I love photography and sports, so this field is perfect for me." DiTrolio hopes to expand his team highlight program to Midwest and far western colleges; his advice for those considering this field: "Learn to relate to people and pick up some business skills through school or college courses and some experience."

A few colleges and a number of private trade/technical schools exist that provide photography training. One such school, Antonelli Institute (Plymouth Meeting, PA) offers a two-year program leading to an associate degree in photography. Students take courses in: Fundamentals of Photography, Color Lab Techniques, Basic Lighting, Video/Electronic Imaging, and others. Students with an interest in sports would focus their class assignments in that direction. Graduates enter a wide range of careers.

For additional information, consider reading *Opportunities in Photography* in the VGM Career Horizons series and writing to:

Photographic Society of America
P.O. Box 1266
Reseda, CA 91335

AGENTS AND SPORTS REPRESENTATIVES

In this era of fantastic salaries for professional athletes, the agent has become a visible member of the sports scene. Agents, sometimes called representatives, act as the players' intermediaries with the team's owner and general manager, to secure the best financial and playing arrangement for the athlete. The use of agents occurs in several professions: For example, writers use literary agents and those in show business use booking agents.

Agents are usually lawyers or accountants. They obtain their salary as a percentage of the income the player will receive from the team (or athletic event, as in boxing). Agents normally receive ten percent for their negotiation of the contract. When one considers the salaries of individuals like Ric Flair, Shaquille O'Neal, Wayne Gretzky, Barry Bonds, and Ryne Sandberg, you realize that this sports career provides an excellent salary.

In addition to negotiating contracts, many serve as financial agents for players, making suggestions for investments, product endorsements, and handling income taxes. Some act as representatives for organizations such as the football players or for baseball umpires. In doing so, they work to obtain better salaries, retirement benefits, and improved working conditions.

Richie Phillips, well-known attorney and representative for several players and coaches as well as the Major League Baseball Umpires Association, believes he plays an important role in negotiating contracts. Phillips feels that the representative lends objectivity to a situation, since the player or management may not be able to evaluate the athlete's contribution to the team, that is, the player's bargaining position. He believes he additionally serves his clients through careful examination of the language of a contract, for example, the wording of no-cut clauses. Following the signing, as the contract goes into effect, Phillips keeps his clients informed on legal developments, such as the free agent rule; he may become involved if a contract breach occurs. If you're interested in the career, attend law school and do a good job for your clients, suggests Phillips.

For many years, players made their own arrangements with team owners. With the introduction of television, rivalries between leagues, and the expansion of players' legal rights, salaries accelerated greatly. Many athletes in past years were underpaid for the performance; today some players are grossly overpaid. Hopefully a leveling of salaries will occur before sports are seriously damaged in terms of public support.

Opportunities for agents in the future will remain small and the salaries will continue to be excellent. If you're interested, the best background is law or accounting. For law, this means four years of college in which you must do well academically and then three years of law school. Accounting will require undergraduate school. While in school, association with sports as a player, writer, or broadcaster will provide excellent experience.

HEALTH AND FITNESS SPECIALISTS

Laura Schiller became fascinated with aerobics through watching programs on ESPN while at Tabb High School (VA). At Tabb she pursued an interest in athletics through cheerleading and playing field hockey. "I was into the athletics thing—when I got into college combining my ten years of dance training and cheerleading into aerobics was a natural." As a college freshman she participated in aerobics classes. By March of that year, she was ready for certification as an instructor. She attended a workshop dealing with information on fitness, anatomy, and related topics. She gained Primary Certification and by April was filling in occasionally as a paid substitute instructor. Her sophomore year she taught 3 to 4 classes a week, and junior year 4 to 5 classes (these were for advanced students).

Wishing to improve her skills, she attended another teacher training course and obtained her Advanced Aerobics Certification; she hopes to attend a Master Aerobic–Step Instructor class for teachers, shortly. "I like the performance aspect—it's a lot of dancing—I like motivating people. In particular I like challenging the class to work hard," states Schiller. "I plan to become a teacher—this would be a nice part-time job and maybe a school club activity. In addition, it shows prospective employers I have a high energy level."

A number of organizations provide certification in this area. Normally these sessions are offered on weekends and provide lecture and demonstration followed by a test. The AAAI–ISMA (American Aerobic Association International–International Sports Medicine Association) offers a range of certifications from Primary Aerobic Instructor Certification through Fitness Expert Certification. Contact the organization at:

AAAI–ISMA
    P.O. Box 633
    Richboro, PA 18954

Another organization providing training for aerobics and fitness instructors is:

National Dance–Exercise Instructor's Training Association
    1503 South Washington Avenue
    Minneapolis, MN 55454

The growth of health clubs and spas, the development of an interest in industry and business in fitness, and an expanded awareness by retirement homes and communities concerning the relationship of exercise and good health has resulted in a need for individuals trained in these areas.

Serious and experienced athletes and sports enthusiasts realize the value of strength training, and that it involves more than just pumping iron. Today, the athlete's training program must be sports specific. That is, a tennis player must develop different muscles and endurance than a professional football lineman.

The professional organization that certifies individuals in this sports medicine specialty is the National Strength and Conditioning Association (NSCA), boasting approximately 15,000 members. The suggestions for training in this association's excellent journals reflect the most recent scientific research. For example, its *Journal of Applied Sports Science Research* in a recent issue contained articles entitled, "Effects of Weighted Implement Training on Throwing Velocity," "Assessing Anaerobic Power in Collegiate Football Players," and "Applications of Electrostimulation in Physical Conditioning: A Review." Another of its periodicals, the *National Strength and Conditioning Association Journal,* contains articles on: "Diving: Upper Body Strength and Conditioning for Divers," "Off-season Strength Training for Basketball," and "The Science of Cross-training: Theory and Application for Peak Performance." In addition, the NSCA provides videotapes, conferences, posters, courses, and checklists which are beneficial to the membership. Perhaps its most valuable contribution to the profession is its program to certify specialists in the field. Certification includes the right to be designated as a CSCS (Certified Strength and Conditioning Specialist). Specialists in strength and conditioning normally work for professional college teams; some work directly with athletes on a consulting basis. Often a sports medicine center or a health and fitness club will utilize the services of these specialists on a part-time basis. This career field will continue to grow as athletes (and the general public) continue to increase their desire for athletic success enhanced by strength training and physical conditioning.

While certification does require as one of its criteria a college degree, some people work successfully without the benefit of a college diploma. These individuals have acquired through study and experience a knowledge of the field. However, specialists in the future will need a college degree to find employment. Few will be hired without certification.

For additional information contact:

The National Strength and Conditioning Association
P.O. Box 81410
Lincoln, NE 68504

Normally health and fitness specialists have come from the ranks of physical education teachers and individuals with an interest in fitness (weight trainers, joggers, aerobic dancers, martial arts followers). However, as this field becomes more specialized and important, the next generation of these career specialists will come largely from the ranks of exercise physiologists.

Health clubs and spas employ a wide variety of individuals with an interest in fitness. Most do not have special training; however, some of the larger, more expensive clubs may employ an exercise specialist. This person would train the other employees, organize the fitness program, and assist members who want advice on health and fitness.

Some business organizations with a strong interest in their employees' physical fitness have built health clubs in their factories and office complexes. To manage these facilities they have hired exercise physiologists. Dr. Ron Feingold, Chairman, Department of Physical Education and Human Performance Science at Adelphi University on Long Island, New York, relates that Adelphi's graduate program in Exercise Physiology has shown excellent growth, attracting students with backgrounds in physical education, nursing, physical therapy, and related areas who all wish to move into this exciting new area. Dr. Feingold believes opportunities will be excellent in the 1990s, particularly for those interested in positions in health clubs associated with businesses.

Some exercise physiologists take positions in retirement homes and communities. These individuals conduct exercise classes, manage the facility, and provide motivation and advice to the residents. Persons interested in this area can take a special master's degree called Exercise Specialist for the Aged, available at some universities.

Salaries for exercise physiologists vary with the position; those in industrial positions and retirement facilities do best, averaging $25,000-$60,000 per year. Health spa employees receive minimal salaries plus commissions; those with advanced degrees in management positions receive $25,000-$100,000 depending upon their level of responsibility.

Those interested in pursuing this career should have an interest in science and athletics, and enjoy working with people. In general, a master's degree will be necessary; undergraduate grades must be very good. Some individuals with a college degree in recreation may enter this profession. This career will undoubtedly be one of the fastest growing jobs in the 1990s; for additional information, write:

American Association of Fitness Directors in
    Business and Industry
700 Anderson Hill Road
Purchase, NY 10577

SPORTS FACILITY MAINTENANCE PERSONNEL

Long before players and fans arrive, the ground crew prepares the fields and arenas for athletic contests not only for games and events, but also for practice.

Sometimes this requires hard work into the early hours of the morning at the busier locations. For example, at New York's Madison Square Garden, the following may happen in 24 hours: an afternoon circus performance, a hockey game that evening, and the following morning basketball practice! At the other end of the spectrum, college stadium or community field maintenance proceeds in a much more leisurely fashion.

Most employees in these positions learn their skills on the job. However, some positions—involving things such as maintaining grass playing fields, equipment, and supervision of employees—require specific knowledge. These individuals may have a degree in recreation or sports management. Opportunities exist in a variety of situations; each town, city, school, college, and professional team has an athletic facility that needs constant maintenance. If you have an interest in a particular sport (soccer, hockey, lacrosse), you may need to move to pursue it as certain sports are played on a regional basis only.

COMPLEMENTARY HEALTH THERAPIES

A strong movement exists in the country toward supporting conventional medicine with complementary strategies such as: acupuncture, sports massage, and nutrition (diet, vitamin, mineral, herbal supplementation). In addition these procedures can have a beneficial effect on maximizing an athlete's performance.

The Pacific College of Oriental Medicine in San Diego offers programs in the area of acupuncture and massage therapy. In the latter area students can take course work in the massage technician curriculum and obtain certification and then move ahead to massage therapy. Studying acupuncture includes study of that technique but also herbology, therapeutic exercise, massage, and Oriental physical therapy. College courses vary in length from several weeks to three years; for a list of colleges with programs contact:

American Association of Acupuncture and Oriental Medicine
1424 16th Street N.W., Suite 501
Washington, DC 20036

Sports massage continues to gain adherents, as with the acupuncture technique. The procedure focuses upon the nature of the athletic activity (tennis players are treated differently than soccer players). Some massage therapists operate a private practice, others work at sports medicine clinics, and many obtain employment at health clubs. For additional information and a list of schools contact:

American Massage Therapy Association
1130 W. North Shore Avenue
Chicago, IL 60626

Athletes long in the forefront of the nutrition movement have sought to "eat and win" and to supplement their diets with vitamins, minerals, and herbs to "gain an edge" over their opponents. Recently the positive research results on optimizing performance with supplementation combined with a strong desire to avoid drugs has enhanced this field among those in athletics.

Professional sports nutritionists may have backgrounds in medicine—physicians, nurses, and others who have obtained additional coursework and certification; others (athletic coaches, physical therapists, etc.) have attended special programs to study nutrition. The latter, while not entitled to be called nutritionists, do assist those in sports with diet suggestions. Some in this field have attended schools emphasizing holistic health and have an array of unproven but promising suggestions for athletes.

Those involved in this growing field work with sports medicine centers or in private practice providing advice to coaches and players. They have strong backgrounds in science (biochemistry in particular) and excellent interpersonal skills. In addition, most have a strong dedication to wellness for themselves and their clients. For additional information read *Sports Nutrition* (Keats Publishing, New Canaan, CT) by Walter Evans, and *Optimum Nutrition for Athletes* (Morrow Publishing, New York) by Michael Colgan; subscribe to *Nutrition and Fitness* magazine, 511 Encinitas Boulevard, Suite 101, Encinitas, CA 90024. The Colgan Institute at this address offers a program leading to certification. Also you may wish to contact:

International Center for Sports Nutrition
    502 South 44th Street
    Suite 3012
    Omaha, NE 68105

An excellent source of information on this entire field of complementary health strategies is the *East-West Natural Health* magazine, 17 Station Street, Brookline Village, MA 02147.

STADIUM AND ARENA CONCESSIONAIRES

One of the most lucrative sports-related occupations involves owning a concession. Generally, they sell everything from hats to peanuts and have little competition.

While few opportunities exist for obtaining a concession stand, some may be available at colleges—these go out for bid from time to time. To obtain a position as vendor, call a local college or professional team. Most likely, the procedure will involve going to the office of the concessionaire and filling out appropriate forms. You may wish to consider becoming a vendor part-time; this job will gain you free admission to the events and enable you to obtain money for saving and spending. It's difficult and hard work carrying boxes around for several hours, many times in hot temperatures, while hawking your wares, but in addition to your salary, you learn patience and hard work.

Previously employed persons receive preference; as those persons leave, others are called. The first to sign up are first called. Sometimes you can get your start when extras are added for big games—those in which attendance will be greater than usual.

Believe it or not, some professional players originally worked selling in the stands before making it big on the playing field. While this might not be the best way to make it in the pros it does permit the opportunity to be close to a sport you love.

To gain insight into this career, read *Recreational Foodservice Management* (Van Nostrand Reinhold) by Mickey Warner. It provides an excellent overview of the industry from event planning and vending management to making a profit.

SPORTS INSTRUCTOR

The expansion of leisure time in our society has witnessed a dramatic growth in lifetime sports . . . these areas, such as personal fitness, golf, tennis, scuba diving, swimming, martial arts, and hiking have developed to the extent that there is a great need for instructors. Frequently called "pros," they teach individuals and small groups everything from a general introduction to the activity to its finer points.

These sports pros have had successful careers and many have developed a following. Several continue to compete, if only regionally, using teaching to supplement their income during the off season. Instructors often are employed by sports facilities such as golf, swimming, or country clubs; some own a "pro shop" which sells sporting equipment. In some cases, they own their own schools and conduct courses there and in the community. For example, a scuba diver, skater, or gymnast, in addition to offering classes at her or his school, will offer courses at the local evening school and community college certain nights of the week.

In preparing for a career in this area, school courses in business, communication arts, and understanding others (history and the social sciences) will provide a good academic background. This must be combined with sports involvement, preferably as a participant. It may be possible in certain areas, as swimming, not to have been a well-known athlete, but to have served as a successful coach. While college is not necessary, it will be helpful. Salaries vary dramatically with the instructors' success and reputation. Those who have authored a popular book, for example, may be frequently quoted in newspapers or generally have a celebrity status and receive excellent salaries for tutoring individuals or consulting with teams.

SPORTS ENTREPRENEUR

Deeply imbedded in the character of North Americans lies the desire to start a business and "be the boss." The fertile soil of democratic capitalism planted with the seeds of a sports idea can produce a wonderful harvest. Nike, Nautilus, ESPN, and Nordic Track exemplify this concept; numerous other examples exist at a smaller scale in all aspects of sports.

Charles Watkins has an idea. He'd like to carve out a niche for his young organization, Management Strategies Unlimited, in the vast world of sports marketing and management. Specifically, he wishes to work with professional players in the area of public relations and career development and represent and assist the marketing of sports products. "It's difficult to start in this industry without capital, but some agents only negotiate player contracts—someone else then needs to pick with [sic] related activities—that's where we fit." Watkins plans also to work with college and high school athletes, obtaining sponsors to undertake basic skill and career development programs. Watkins represents one of the millions who wish to marry their love of sports with a personal expertise and develop a career.

The range of potential entrepreneurial activities can be seen from the talents of the team entitled the "California Girls!" Stacy Anderson and her partner Amy Bekkan have turned their success at Frisbee into a career. They have appeared on television, in magazines and newspapers, on sports halftime shows, at special events, at parties, and at sports trade shows worldwide. Amy has dominated disc competition in the U.S. and has repeatedly won every major title, virtually dominating the sport. Her partner Stacy, a former competitive swimmer with a background in dance, has taken first place in national freestyle disc competition. Together they have given seminars and demonstrations in Tokyo and competed in Australia. Presently they combine prospecting for appearances with practice. Amy is listed in the *Guiness Book of World Records* for powering a Frisbee 141 meters! She hopes to better that mark some day. Stacy continues to perfect her dance routines. They want to achieve their ultimate goal: as the main attraction of a halftime show for the NFL's Super Bowl.

Other sports entrepreneurs range from individuals who run the corner baseball card and memorabilia shop to the businessperson who starts a professional wrestling school to the computer specialist who designs programs to improve the visual acuity of an athlete.

The expanding world of sports and athletics provides ample opportunity for the sports entrepreneur.

STATISTICIANS

Statistics no longer exist just for "sports trivia fans." Coaches have expanded their interest in this area. The computer has emerged as a weapon in the arsenal. The data supplied by the computer add to the coach's knowledge of her or his team or the opponent, providing information that can assist with decision making. For example, the computer can process a great deal of data and find patterns. Football scouts can provide the computer with statistics on an opposing team, and then program it to provide information such as what play the team tends to run in a given situation, for example, when losing in the fourth quarter, the opposing team has a tendency to pass to the tight end on third down.

Statistics are kept at most levels of play. Which information is kept depends for the most part upon the philosophy of the coach. Using basketball, one coach may only want rebounding statistics on her or his players; another may keep shot charts (location of shots taken) and turnovers (the number, and which players lost the ball to the other team) and still others keep vast amounts of information on their team and others. This may include such detailed information in a scouting report as the number of passes made between each player during a basketball game. Many high school coaches record extra statistics, those over and above the information kept by the official scorer.

The coach at this level can be greatly aided by a competent student statistician; likewise the student can gain valuable experience. Normally the coach will have a prepared form on which to record the information. The coach will explain the procedures to be followed and will allow the aspiring statistician to gain some experience in intrasquad and preseason scrimmages. Once the season begins, the coach will expect perfect accuracy. College students may wish to approach a coach at their school about aiding a team with statistics. Experience will prove helpful. If you lack the background you may wish to practice taking "stats" when watching a game or event. While this is quite minimal it might convince a coach of your desire to serve as a statistician. A knowledge of personal computers, data entry, and programming will prove beneficial.

Careers as a sports statistician remain quite limited on a full-time basis; however, several opportunities do exist to follow this job as an avocation. It should be mentioned that developing some skill in this area will prove beneficial in related areas such as sports information and newspaper careers.

SPORTS CARTOONIST

His work appears in the sports section of over 150 newspapers and sometimes without writing a word!

Steve Moore, creator of "In the Bleachers," a sports cartoon, began cartooning as a college student at Oregon State University. He continued his art with local newspapers as a graduate student while at Oregon State. Eventually his interest in sports cartooning evolved into its present format. He explains, "It seemed to me that sports were being taken so seriously—like big business. 'In the Bleachers' is my way of putting some fun back into the game." Moore shares his art humor with sports page readers from LA *(LA Times)* to Washington, DC, *(Washington Times)* and in between—*Crystal Lake* (IL) *Herald* and the *Fort Worth Star Telegram.*

Other sports cartoonists work their magic around the country—Stephen Mellus "Draft Choices" (*Middletown* (NY) *Record*); Vic Harville *(Arkansas Democrat–Gazette);* and the dean of the art form, Bill Gallo *(NY Daily News).*

Sports cartooning represents the extent to which sports have permeated all aspects of our society. As a career option, opportunities exist largely on a part-time basis. If the field interests you, start on a small scale with your local school or college newspaper. Improve your skills and build a track record and circulate your "stuff" to prospect for other purchasers (magazines/newspapers). Your skill and some luck may result in a national audience!

SCOUT

Scouts' decisions affect players, coaches, and games more than most people realize. Scouts are sports intelligence agents. Scouting takes two forms: evaluating potential players and studying future opponents.

At the college level, players are chosen to fill the ranks of the team. Consequently, college coaches (even at small colleges) continually assess high school athletes; those of exceptional ability are offered scholarships. The selection of the correct person contributes to team success. Inability to make the appropriate selection may result in the firing of the coach. College scouts attend high school games, read magazines and newspapers, and get letters from alumni. To identify potential players, the real talent comes in judging which will truly become stars or superstars. Usually an assistant is designated to serve as a head scout; some free-lance scouts exist. These aid colleges by providing individual reports to specific coaches and general publications evaluating players' abilities.

Another area of scouting involves observing opponents' teams to prepare to play them. In this case, the scout records the system used and players' abilities and tendencies; specific details are extremely important. The information obtained forms the basis of the scouting report distributed to the coaching staff and team. Again, most of this work is performed by the school's coaches. However, some individuals and small companies do scouting on an independent basis.

At the professional level, scouting follows a similar structure, but is of an even more serious nature. For example, the Cincinnati Reds have 18 full-time scouts, plus 15 part-time and 300 recommending scouts. In addition, they subscribe to a daily report on prospects prepared by the Major League Scouting Bureau. The Dallas Cowboys have named their scouting department the War Room!

In locating new talent there exists great secrecy so as not to tip off an opponent to your interest. For example, the Boston Celtics basketball team had a strong interest in collegian Dave Cowan (who later became a Celtic great) which they did not want to reveal. While watching one of his college games at Florida State University, the Celtics' scout waited for Cowan to make a mistake, then he walked out shaking his head. Cowan was drafted by Boston and served as an excellent player and even coached.

Often most teams know of the "Blue Chip" player; therefore, the real test of a scout is to locate the "sleeper": the late-blooming player who, with proper coaching, will develop into the superstar. It is the sleeper player who must be kept a secret; Joe Bowen, head scout for the Reds baseball team, believes that scouting is like any other kind of espionage: if your secrets aren't airtight, you're out of business.

The detail involved in scouting is far greater than is generally realized; for example, in evaluating potential players the Dallas Cowboys football team uses 40 characteristics, including 12 types of thighs and 9 kinds of hands.

Similarly, great time and effort go into the scout's measuring opposing teams and preparing game plans. Films and videotapes provide the opportunity to carefully scrutinize the opposition.

More opportunities exist for scouting positions in professional sports than in college ranks. The job would involve employment with a team or scouting organization.

Before you jump into this career read carefully *Prophets of the Sandlots* (by Mark Winegardner), which tells the story of Tony Lucadello, perhaps the greatest of all baseball scouts. Lucadello traveled over two million miles in the United States and Canada watching future prospects, locating 49 who made it to the major leagues! However, while rewarding, this is not an easy life and clearly only for those dedicated few.

Preparation for scouting careers at any level involves expert knowledge of physical and psychological ability. Most scouts are former players and coaches. Salaries are good to very good, but for most, the reward is knowing that you located another superstar.

SPORTS ACADEMICIANS

In addition to college instructors who teach courses in professional areas (physical education, sports management, physical therapy), the expansion of programs related to sports studies, sports health sciences, and related courses on college campuses has created a need for expanded faculty.

In recent years several scholars have begun to examine various aspects of sports from the perspective of their academic areas of study. These individuals have approached athletics and organized sports in systematic ways, armed with an excellent knowledge of how to conduct in-depth studies of a particular topic. In addition, they prepare courses of study for teaching.

Sports historians examine areas such as the biographies of famous athletes or trends from past decades such as the origin of a sport. They also work to encourage high school teachers to incorporate athletics into their courses when teaching U.S. history. Frequently, these individuals publish articles in the *Journal of Sports History* (published at the Pennsylvania State University) for the appreciation of the reader and the expansion of knowledge.

Some sociologists have studied the role of sports in society. For example, they investigate topics such as racial problems, attitudes toward winning and losing, and the effect money has had upon athletes. Like other academic persons, most sociologists teach in colleges. Those with a special interest in athletics frequently offer courses with titles such as Sociology of Sport and Sport in American Society.

Running Therapy, Mental Toughness, the Psychology of Coaching are some of the topics of interest to sport psychologists. These individuals have a particular interest in the mental aspects of athletics. Frequently, they provide guidance to players and coaches concerning how they achieve greater success through closer attention to the psychological aspects of athletics. For coaches this means subjects such as motivation and the establishment of smooth working relationships with players; for the players, it means areas such as mental aspects of relaxation and of pregame preparation. (See also section on sports psychology.)

Philosophers with an eye toward sports have involved themselves in teaching courses and writing for the *Journal for the Philosophy of Sport*.

Most jobs in the area of sports academicians exist at the university level. This means that if you have an interest in this area you will need to attend college at the undergraduate level and then graduate school until you obtain a doctorate. A love of reading and scholarly activity is important as well as an ongoing desire to add to the body of knowledge of sports. Interested? Perhaps someday you may teach a course entitled The Contribution of Athletics to American Culture or Management

Techniques for Sports Facilities or conduct research on The Mental Aspects of Pregame Preparation or The Value of Sports in a Small Town.

EQUIPMENT MANAGER

For those without a college degree, what is the fastest-growing career in sports and athletics?

The person responsible for the handling and care of everything from bats to helmets is the equipment manager. This profession offers opportunities for employment largely at the college and professional levels. The equipment manager has the responsibility of keeping the team's equipment cleaned and in good repair, having the equipment available for practice and games (this means traveling with the team), and providing security for the equipment. The last serves as the greatest problem of the equipment manager. Often this person is aided at the professional level by an assistant and at the college level by the teams' student managers. Often he or she will aid the team with other tasks as necessary.

Persons employed in this profession normally have a great interest in the sport with which they are associated; often they have played or coached. Some have served as salespersons of sports equipment. While no special training or education is necessary, a knowledge of the equipment and the ability to perform minor repairs is important. Also, the personal qualities of reliability and punctuality are a must.

Although equipment managers have been actively performing the craft for over 100 years, their professional organization has existed for only a few years. Presently salaries are attractive. Those at the college level earn salaries in the $18,000 to $32,000 range; at the professional level, from $22,000 to $50,000. Bob Lambert, presently equipment manager at Villanova University, has also served at the professional level. He enjoys this job because it keeps him close to sports and allows him to travel. Lambert proclaims, "The job opportunities are great and it's a wide-open area for women." For further information, contact:

The Equipment Managers Association
Bowling Green State University
Bowling Green, OH 43402

FUTURE CAREERS

In addition to the many careers mentioned directly or indirectly in this book, some new careers will develop and grow in importance in the decades ahead. The following are examples.

In the last few years some teams in the National Football League have obtained the services of *agility and strength* coaches. These specialists are responsible for improving players by making them stronger, quicker, and less susceptible to injury. They use weight training, agility exercises, and various drills specifically designed to improve a player relative to her or his position. In Philadelphia, Ernie Mao, a 5'8'' 158-pounder, provides strength and conditioning guidance to the football players on the Eagles. He is testimony that professionals in athletics come in all sizes. Mao works part time with the Eagles; his full-time position is supervisor of youth activities for the PAL (Police Athletic League).

In the years ahead, significantly more attention will be paid to this area at all levels of athletics. In many cases (particularly at the professional level) it will come in the form of one full-time person but in most cases it will be a coach who has other duties but has special expertise in these areas.

Some human performance specialists serve on university faculties in departments and schools of physical education. While this will continue there exists a noticeable trend toward the involvement of these specialists in athletic laboratories and as consultants of individuals, teams, sporting goods companies, and health spas. One such example is Dr. Marvin I. Clein of the University of Denver's Human Performance Laboratory. Working with a team of exercise physiologists and psychologists, they evaluate the potential of athletes: Do they have the mental ability and the physical body to succeed at the sport they wish to play? This scientific approach attempts to identify future champions and/or isolate weaknesses of athletes so as to design strategies for improvement. In this regard, it is nice to know that some outstanding players, whom no one ever guessed would make it to the professional ranks, have done so, because of great desire and hard work.

Other sports and athletics-related careers primed to undergo expansion include: dance therapist, kinesiologist, adaptive physical education teacher, *naturapathic* doctor and *therapeutic recreation specialist*. Stay alert to their development and the emergence of new ones.

Sports careers will expand, change, and grow depending upon the interests of fans, players, coaches, and others. Observe these trends so you can take advantage of the constantly changing and expanding opportunities in the wonderful world of sports and athletics.

SPORTS AND ATHLETICS ORGANIZATIONS

The following organizations can offer information relative to the sport or activity with which they are associated. Many will be able to provide dates of contests, requirements for certain jobs, and additional locations for information you may wish. These are in alphabetical order by association emphasis.

NATIONAL ARCHERY
ASSOCIATION OF THE
UNITED STATES (NAA)
1750 E. Boulder Street
Colorado Springs, CO 80909
(303) 569–6900

AMATEUR ATHLETIC UNION OF
THE UNITED STATES (AAU)
3400 W. 86th Street
Indianapolis, IN 46268
(317) 297–2900

ATHLETES IN ACTION
4790 Irvine Blvd.
Suite 105–325
Irvine, CA 92711
(714) 669–1720

COLLEGE ATHLETIC BUSINESS
MANAGERS ASSOCIATION
(CABMA)
Baylor University
Box 6427
Waco, TX 76706
(817) 754–4648

NATIONAL JUNIOR COLLEGE
ATHLETIC ASSOCIATION
(NJCAA)
P.O. Box 1586
Hutchinson, KS 67501
(316) 663–5445

NATIONAL ASSOCIATION OF
INTERCOLLEGIATE
ATHLETICS (NAIA)
221 Baltimore
Kansas City, MO 64105
(816) 842–5050

NATIONAL COLLEGIATE
ATHLETIC ASSOCIATION
(NCAA)
Nall Avenue at 63rd Street
P.O. Box 1906
Shawnee Mission, KS 66222
(913) 384–3220

UNITED STATES AUTO CLUB
(USAC)
4910 W. 16th Street
Indianapolis, IN 46224
(317) 247–5151

AMERICAN AMATEUR
BASEBALL CONGRESS
(AABC)
212 Plaza Bldg.
2855 W. Market Street
Akron, OH 44313
(216) 836–6424

AMERICAN ASSOCIATION OF
COLLEGE BASEBALL
COACHES (AACBC)
605 Hamilton Drive
Champaign, IL 61820
(217) 356–6811

ASSOCIATION OF
PROFESSIONAL BALL
PLAYERS OF AMERICA
(BASEBALL) (APBPA)
12062 Valley View St.,
Suite 211
Garden Grove, CA 92645
(714) 892–9900

LITTLE LEAGUE BASEBALL
Williamsport, PA 17701
(717) 326–1921

NATIONAL ASSOCIATION OF
LEAGUES, UMPIRES AND
SCORERS (BASEBALL)
(NALUS)
Box 1420
Wichita, KS 67201
(316) 267–7333

NATIONAL ASSOCIATION OF
PROFESSIONAL BASEBALL
LEAGUES (NAPBL)
P.O. Box A
225 Fourth Street, S.E.
St. Petersburg, FL 33731
(813) 822–6937

NATIONAL BASEBALL
CONGRESS (NBS)
Box 1420
Wichita, KS 67201
(316) 267–7333

INTERNATIONAL ASSOCIATION
OF APPROVED
BASKETBALL OFFICIALS
(IAABO)
P.O. Box 661
West Hartford, CT 06107
(203) 232–7530

NATIONAL ASSOCIATION OF
BASKETBALL COACHES OF
THE UNITED STATES
(NABC)
P.O. Box 307
Branford, CT 06405
(203) 488–1232

AMATEUR BICYCLE
ASSOCIATION OF AMERICA
924 Cherry Street
San Carlos, CA 94070

AMERICAN BILLIARD
  ASSOCIATION (ABA)
1660 Lin Lor Ct.
Elgin, IL 60120
(708) 741–6836

AMERICAN BOWLING
  CONGRESS (ABC)
5301 S. 76th Street
Greendale, WI 53129
(414) 421–6400

AMERICAN JUNIOR BOWLING
  CONGRESS (AJBC)
5301 S. 76th Street
Greendale, WI 53129
(414) 421–4700

PROFESSIONAL BOWLERS
  ASSOCIATION OF AMERICA
  (BOWLING) (PBA)
1720 Merriman Road
Akron, OH 44313
(216) 836–5568

WOMEN'S INTERNATIONAL
  BOWLING CONGRESS
  (WIBC)
5301 S. 76th Street
Greendale, WI 53129
(414) 421–4700

GOLDEN GLOVES ASSOCIATION
  OF AMERICA (BOXING)
1704 Moon Avenue
Albuquerque, NM 87112
(505) 294–8659

INTERNATIONAL VETERAN
  BOXERS ASSOCIATION
  (IVBA)
94 Crescent Ave.
New Rochelle, NY 10801
(914) 235–0955

INTERNATIONAL
  CHEERLEADING
  FOUNDATION (ICF)
4425 Indian Creek Parking
Overland Park, KS 66207
(913) 649–3666

NATIONAL HIGH SCHOOL
  ATHLETIC COACHES
  ASSOCIATION (NHSACA)
3423 E. Silver Springs Blvd.,
  Suite Nine
Ocala, FL 32670
(904) 622–3660

SPORT FISHING INSTITUTE (SFI)
608 13th Street, N.W.
Washington, DC 20005
(202) 737–0668

AMERICAN FOOTBALL
  COACHES ASSOCIATION
  (AFCA)
Tangerine Sports
Pan American Bank Bldg.
250 N. Orange, Suite 300
Orlando, FL 38801
(305) 423–2476

CANADIAN FOOTBALL LEAGUE
  PLAYERS ASSOCIATION
1686 Albert Street
Regina, Saskatchewan, Canada
  S4P 256
(306) 525–2158

FOOTBALL WRITERS
  ASSOCIATION OF AMERICA
  (FWAA)
Box 1022
Edmond, OK 73034
(405) 341–4731

NATIONAL FOOTBALL
FOUNDATION AND HALL
OF FAME (NFF)
201 E. 42nd St., Suite 1506
New York, NY 10017
(212) 682–6943

NATIONAL FOOTBALL LEAGUE
(NFL)
410 Park Avenue
New York, NY 10022
(212) 758–1500

POP WARNER JUNIOR LEAGUE
FOOTBALL
1315 Walnut Street, Suite 606
Philadelphia, PA 19107
(215) 735–1450

PROFESSIONAL FOOTBALL
WRITERS OF AMERICA
(PFWA)
Baton Rouge State Times
4758 Marque Drive
New Orleans, LA 70127
(504) 242–4054

GOLF COACHES ASSOCIATON
OF AMERICA
Bowling Green University
Bowling Green, OH 43403
(419) 372–2876

GOLF WRITERS ASSOCIATION
OF AMERICA (GWAA)
P.O. Box 37324
Cincinnati, OH 45222
(513) 631–4400

PROFESSIONAL
GOLFERS' ASSOCIATION OF
AMERICA (PGA)
Box 12458
Palm Beach Gardens, FL 33410
(305) 626–3600

NATIONAL ASSOCIATION OF
COLLEGIATE GYMNASTICS
COACHES (NACGC)
% Athletic Department
Temple University
Philadelphia, PA 19122
(215) 787–7452

INTERNATIONAL COMMITTEE
OF SPORTS FOR THE DEAF
(HANDICAPPED)
Gallaudet College
Washington, DC 20002
(202) 651–5114

NATIONAL HANDICAPPED
SPORTS AND RECREATION
ASSOCIATION (NHSRA)
P.O. Box 18664, Capitol Hill
Station
Denver, CO 80218
(303) 978–0564

AMATEUR HOCKEY
ASSOCIATION OF THE
UNITED STATES (AHAUS)
2997 Broadmoor Valley Road
Colorado Springs, CO 80906
(303) 576–4990

AMERICAN HOCKEY LEAGUE
(AHL)
31 Elm Street, Suite 533
Springfield, MA 01103
(413) 781–2030

NATIONAL HOCKEY LEAGUE
(NHL)
920 Sun Life Bldg.
Montreal, PQ, Canada H3B 2W2
(514) 871–9220

AMERICAN TRAINERS
ASSOCIATION (HORSE
RACING) (ATA)
P.O. Box 6702
Towson, MD 21204
(301) 828–4531

JOCKEY'S GUILD (HORSE
RACING) (JG)
55 Fifth Ave., Rm. 1501
New York, NY 10017
(212) 687–7746

THOROUGHBRED CLUB OF
AMERICA (HORSE RACING)
(TCA)
P.O. Box 8147
Lexington, KY 40533
(606) 277–8202

UNITED STATES HARNESS
WRITERS' ASSOCIATION
(HORSE RACING) (USHWA)
P.O. Box 10
Batavia, NY 14020
(716) 344–1490

UNITED STATES TROTTING
ASSOCIATION (HORSE
RACING) (USTA)
750 Michigan Avenue
Columbus, OH 43215
(614) 224–2291

UNITED THOROUGHBRED
TRAINERS OF AMERICA
(HORSE RACING) (UTTA)
19363 James Couzens Highway
Detroit, MI 48235
(313) 342–6144

UNITED STATES AMATEUR JAI
ALAI PLAYERS
ASSOCIATION
44 Brickell Avenue
Miami, FL 33131
(305) 377–3333

THE LACROSSE FOUNDATION
Newton H. White, Jr. Athletic
Center
Homewood
Baltimore, MD 21218
(301) 235–6882

UNITED STATES OLYMPIC
COMMITTEE (USOC)
1750 E. Boulder Street
Colorado Springs, CO 80909
(303) 632–5551

NATIONAL PADDLEBALL
ASSOCIATION (NPA)
P.O. Box 712
Flint, MI 48501
(313) 742–6274

UNITED STATES MODERN
PENTATHLON AND
BIATHLON ASSOCIATION
(USMPBA)
1600 Rhode Island Avenue, N.W.
Washington, DC 20036
(202) 828–6222

PEOPLE-TO-PEOPLE SPORTS
  COMMITTEE
98 Cutter Mill Road
Great Neck, NY 11021
  (516) 482–5158

ASSOCIATION OF PHYSICAL
  FITNESS CENTERS
600 Jefferson Street, Suite 202
Rockville, MD 20852
  (301) 424–7744

ACADEMY FOR THE
  PSYCHOLOGY OF SPORTS
  INTERNATIONAL (APSI)
2062 Arlington Avenue
Toledo, OH 43609
  (419) 385–0044

NORTH AMERICAN SOCIETY
  FOR THE PSYCHOLOGY OF
  SPORT AND PHYSICAL
  ACTIVITY (NASPSPA)
Department of Athletics
Louisiana State University
Baton Rouge, LA 70803
  (504) 388–2015

COLLEGE SPORTS
  INFORMATION DIRECTORS
  OF AMERICA (PUBLIC
  RELATIONS) (CoSIDA)
Campus Box 114
Texas A & I University
Kingsville, TX 78363
  (512) 595–3908

UNITED STATES RACQUETBALL
  ASSOCIATION (USRA)
4101 Dempster St.
Skokie, IL 60076
  (708) 673–4000

PROFESSIONAL RODEO
  COWBOYS ASSOCIATION
  (PRCA)
101 Prorodeo Drive
Colorado Springs, CO 80901
  (303) 593–8840

AMERICAN SKI TEACHERS
  ASSOCIATION OF NATUR
  TEKNIK (ASTAN)
R.D. 5 Bingen Road
Bethlehem, PA 18015
  (215) 867–8265

PROFESSIONAL SKI
  INSTRUCTORS OF AMERICA
  (PSIA)
3333 Iris
Boulder, CO 80301
  (303) 447–0842

UNITED STATES SKI WRITERS
  ASSOCIATION (USSWA)
P.O. Box 100
Park City, UT 84060
  (801) 649–9090

NATIONAL INTERCOLLEGIATE
  SOCCER OFFICIALS
  ASSOCIATION (NISOA)
131 Moffitt Blvd.
Islip, NY 11751
  (516) 277–3878

NATIONAL SOCCER COACHES
  ASSOCIATION OF AMERICA
  (NSCA)
R.D. #5
Box 5074
Stoudsburg, PA 18360
  (717) 421–8720

NATIONAL SOCCER LEAGUE
(NSL)
4534 N. Lincoln Avenue
Chicago, IL 60625
(312) 275–2850

AMERICAN ORTHOPAEDIC
SOCIETY FOR SPORTS
MEDICINE
2250 E. Devon Avenue, Suite 115
Des Plaines, IL 60018
(708) 803–8700

AMERICAN OSTEOPATHIC
ACADEMY OF SPORTS
MEDICINE
P.O. Box 623
Middleton, WI 53562
(608) 831–4400

NATIONAL ACADEMY OF
SPORTS
220 E. 63rd Street
New York, NY 10021
(212) 838–5860

CANADIAN NATIONAL SPORTS
AND RECREATION CENTRE
1600 James Naismith Drive
Gloucester, Ontario, Canada KIB
5N4
(613) 746–0060

NATIONAL SPORTSCASTERS
AND SPORTSWRITERS
ASSOCIATION
P.O. Drawer 559
Salisbury, NC 28745
(704) 633–4275

SPORTS TURF MANAGERS
ASSOCIATION
P.O. Box 94657
Las Vegas, NV 40503
(606) 277–8202

AMERICAN SURFING
ASSOCIATION (ASA)
Box 2622
Newport Beach, CA 92663
(714) 760–7073

AMERICAN SWIMMING
COACHES ASSOCIATION
(ASCA)
One Hall of Fame Drive
Ft. Lauderdale, FL 33316
(305) 462–6267

INTERCOLLEGIATE TENNIS
COACHES ASSOCIATION
Athletic Department
Clemson University
Clemson, SC 29631
(803) 656–2101

UNITED STATES PROFESSIONAL
TENNIS ASSOCIATION
(USPTA)
P.O. Box 1659
Sarasota, FL 33578
(813) 383–5555

UNITED STATES TENNIS
ASSOCIATION (USTA)
51 E. 42nd Street
New York, NY 10017
(212) 949–9110

THE ATHLETICS
  CONGRESS/USA (TRACK)
  (TAC/USA)
P.O. Box 120
Indianapolis, IN 46206
  (317) 638–9155

PROFESSIONAL ASSOCIATION
  OF DIVING INSTRUCTORS
  (UNDERWATER) (PADI)
1243 E. Warner Avenue
Santa Ana, CA 92705
  (714) 540–7234

UNITED STATES VOLLEYBALL
  ASSOCIATION (USVBA)
1750 E. Boulder
Colorado Springs, CO 80909
  (303) 632–5551

NATIONAL WRESTLING
  COACHES ASSOCIATION
% Athletic Department
University of Utah
Salt Lake City, UT 84112
  (801) 581–3527

SPORTS AND ATHLETICS ORGANIZATIONS FOR THOSE WITH SPECIAL NEEDS

AMERICAN ATHLETIC
ASSOCIATION FOR THE
DEAF
1134 Davenport Drive
Burton, MI 49529
(313) 239–3969

AMERICAN BLIND BOWLING
ASSOCIATION
67 Bame Avenue
Buffalo, NY 14215
(716) 863–1472

AMERICAN WHEELCHAIR
BOWLING ASSOCIATION
Larkspur Lane
Menomonee Falls, WI 53501
(914) 781–6876

AMPUTEE SPORTS
ASSOCIATION
P.O. Box 60412
Savannah, GA 31420
(912) 927–5406

BLIND OUTDOOR LEISURE
DEVELOPMENT
533 E. Main Street
Aspen, CO 81611
(303) 925–8922

BLIND SPORTS ASSOCIATION
1939 16th Avenue
San Francisco, CA 94116
(415) 681–1939

CANADIAN DEAF SPORTS
ASSOCIATION
218–1367 W. Broadway
Vancouver, B.C., Canada V6H
4A9
(604) 737–3041 Voice
(604) 738–7122 TDD

CANADA FEDERATION OF
SPORTS ORGANIZATIONS
FOR THE DISABLED
1600 James Naismith Drive
Gloucester, Ontario, Canada K1B
5N4
(613) 748–5630

CANADIAN SPECIAL OLYMPICS
40 St. Clair Avenue West
Toronto, Ontario, Canada M4V
1M6
(416) 928–8100

NATIONAL ASSOCIATION FOR
DISABLED ATHLETES
17 Lindley Avenue
Tenafly, NJ 07670
(201) 236–6560

NATIONAL ASSOCIATION OF
SPORTS FOR CEREBRAL
PALSY
66 East 34th Street
New York, NY 10016
(203) 562–1821

NATIONAL DEAF BOWLING
ASSOCIATION
9244 E. Mansfield Avenue
Denver, CO 80237
(303) 771–9018

NATIONAL HANDICAPPED
SPORTS & RECREATION
ASSOCIATION
1145 19th Street N.W.
Washington, DC 20036
(202) 652–7505

NATIONAL WHEELCHAIR
ATHLETIC ASSOCIATION
3595 E. Fountain Blvd.
Colorado Springs, CO 80910
(719) 547–1150

NATIONAL WHEELCHAIR
BASKETBALL ASSOCIATION
University of Kentucky
110 Seaton Bldg.
Lexington, KY 40506
(606) 257–1623

NORTH AMERICAN
WHEELCHAIR ATHLETIC
ASSOCIATION
P.O. Box 32
Waynesboro, VA 22980
(703) 949–6320

U.S. AMPUTEE ATHLETIC
ASSOCIATION
P.O. Box 210709
Nashville, TN 37221
(615) 662–2323

U.S. ASSOCIATION FOR BLIND
ATHLETES
4708 46th Street N.W.
Washington, DC 20016
(202) 363–1807

U.S. CEREBRAL PALSY
ATHLETIC ASSOCIATION
34518 Warren Road
Suite 264
Westland, MI 48185
(313) 425–8961

U.S. DEAF SKIERS
ASSOCIATION
159 Davis Drive
Hackensack, NJ 07601
(201) 489–3777 (TDD)

SPORTS MUSEUMS AND HALLS OF FAME

Many fine museums and halls of fame exist in the United States and Canada that offer exciting exhibits of sports and athletics. A visit can provide an excellent opportunity to expand your knowledge of a sport that interests you. For example, the Green Bay Packer Football Hall of Fame in Green Bay, Wisconsin, has fourteen major exhibits. Historic and contemporary films, the opportunity to kick a field goal, and old and new equipment are some of the hall's attractions.

The following is an abridged list of some of the sports museums and halls of fame, with addresses and telephone numbers.

AMATEUR SPORTS HALL OF
    FAME
211 Bedford Street
Johnstown, PA 15901
(814) 535–5161

AQUATIC HALL OF FAME AND
    MUSEUM OF CANADA, INC.
436 Main Street
Winnipeg, Manitoba, Canada
R3B 1B2
(204) 947–0131

BERMUDA SPORTS HALL OF
    FAME
Box 121
Hamilton, Bermuda
(809) 295–3434

BRITISH COLUMBIA SPORTS
    HALL OF FAME AND
    MUSEUM
P.O. Box 69020, Station K
Vancouver, B.C., Canada V5K
4W3
(604) 687–5523

CANADA'S SPORTS HALL OF
    FAME
Exhibition Place
Toronto, Ontario, Canada M6K
    SC3

CANADIAN FOOTBALL HALL
    OF FAME
58 Jackson Street West
Hamilton, Ontario, Canada L8P
    1L4

FIRST INTERSTATE ATHLETIC
    FOUNDATION
P.O. Box 60310, Terminal Annex
Los Angeles, CA 90060
(213) 614–2995

FLORIDA SPORTS HALL OF
    FAME
P.O. Box 1847
Lake City, FL 32055
(904) 755–5666

GREATER CLEVELAND SPORTS
    HALL OF FAME
    FOUNDATION, INC.
1375 Euclid Avenue, Suite 412
Cleveland, OH 44115
(216) 781–0678

GREEN BAY PACKER HALL OF
    FAME
1901 South Oneida
Green Bay, WI 54303
(414) 499–4281

GREYHOUND HALL OF FAME
407 South Buckey
Abilene, KS 67410
(913) 263–3000

HOCKEY HALL OF FAME
Exhibition Place
Toronto, Ontario, Canada M6K
    3C3
(416) 595–1345

INDIANA FOOTBALL HALL OF
    FAME
P.O. Box 1035
Richmond, IN 47374
(317) 966–2235

INDIANAPOLIS MOTOR
    SPEEDWAY FOUNDATION
P.O. Box 24152
Speedway, IN 46224
(317) 248–6747

INTERNATIONAL JEWISH
    SPORTS HALL OF FAME
1150 W. Olympic Blvd.
Suite 303
Los Angeles, CA 90064
(213) 276–1014

INTERNATIONAL PALACE OF
    SPORTS, INC.
P.O. Box 332
North Webster, IN 46555
(219) 834–7060

INTERNATIONAL SOFTBALL
    CONGRESS HALL OF FAME
9800 South Sepulveda Blvd.
Los Angeles, CA 90045
(213) 670–7550

INTERNATIONAL SWIMMING
    HALL OF FAME
One Hall of Fame Drive
Fort Lauderdale, FL 33316
(305) 462–6536

INTERNATIONAL TENNIS HALL
OF FAME AND TENNIS
MUSEUM
194 Bellevue Avenue
Newport, RI 02840
(401) 846–4567

INTERNATIONAL WOMEN'S
SPORTS HALL OF FAME
342 Madison Avenue, Suite 728
New York, NY 10173

LITTLE LEAGUE BASEBALL
MUSEUM
P.O. Box 3485
Williamsport, PA 17701
(717) 326–3607

ITALIAN AMERICAN SPORTS
HALL OF FAME
7906 West Grand Avenue
Elmwood Park, IL 60635
(312) 452–4812

LACROSSE FOUNDATION, INC.,
AND LACROSSE HALL OF
FAME
Newton H. White Athletic Center
Homewood
Baltimore, MD 21218
(301) 235–6882

MANITOBA SPORTS HALL OF
FAME
1700 Ellice Avenue
Winnipeg, Manitoba, Canada
R3H OB1
(204) 786–5641

NAISMITH MEMORIAL
BASKETBALL HALL OF
FAME
1050 West Columbus Avenue
Springfield, MA 01101
(413) 781–6500

NATIONAL BASEBALL HALL OF
FAME AND MUSEUM
P.O. Box 590
Cooperstown, NY 13326
(607) 547–9988

NATIONAL BOWLING HALL OF
FAME & MUSEUM, INC.
5301 S. 76th Street
Greendale, WI 53129
(414) 421–6400

NCAA-VISITORS CENTER
6201 College Park
Overland Park, KS 66211
(913) 339–0000

NATIONAL COWBOY HALL OF
FAME
1700 N.E. Street
Oklahoma City, OK 73111
(405) 478–2250

NATIONAL FOOTBALL
FOUNDATION & HALL OF
FAME
201 East 42nd Street, Suite 1506
New York, NY 10017
(212) 682–0255

NATIONAL FOOTBALL
FOUNDATION AND HALL
OF FAME
Kings Island, OH 45034
(513) 241–5410

NATIONAL FRESH WATER
  FISHING HALL OF FAME
Box 33, Hall of Fame Drive
Hayward, WI 54843
(715) 634–4440

NATIONAL HIGH SCHOOL
  SPORTS HALL OF FAME
11724 Plaza Circle, Box 20626
Kansas City, MO 64195
(816) 464–5400

NATIONAL POLISH-AMERICAN
  SPORTS HALL OF FAME &
  MUSEUM
% 9131 Grayfield Avenue
Detroit, MI 48239
(313) 535–206

NATIONAL SKI HALL OF FAME
Box 191
Ishpeming, MI 49849
(906) 486–9281

NATIONAL SPORTSCASTERS
  AND SPORTSWRITERS
  HALL OF FAME
322 E. Innes Street
Salisbury, NC 23144
(704) 633–4275

NATIONAL SOARING MUSEUM,
  INC.
Harris Hill, R.D. No. 1
Elmira, NY 14903
(607) 734–3128

NATIONAL SOFTBALL HALL OF
  FAME & MUSEUM
2801 N.E. 50th Street
Oklahoma City, OK 73111
(405) 424–5267

NATIONAL TRACK & FIELD
  HALL OF FAME OF THE
  U.S.A.
P.O. Box 120
Indianapolis, IN 46206
(317) 638–9155

NATIONAL WRESTLING HALL
  OF FAME
405 West Hall of Fame Avenue
Stillwater, OK 74074
(405) 377–5243

NEW BRUNSWICK SPORTS
  HALL OF FAME
P.O. Box 6000, Queen Street
Fredericton, N.B., Canada E3B
  5H1
(506) 453–3747

NEWFOUNDLAND SPORTS
  HALL OF FAME
Rm. 18 Colonial Building,
  Military Road
St. John's, Newfoundland,
  Canada A1C 2C9
(709) 753–8613

NEW ENGLAND MUSEUM OF
  SPORTS
1175 Soldiers Field Road
Boston, MA 02134
(617) 782–2692

NEW JERSEY SPORTS HALL OF
  FAME
Sports and Exposition Authority
East Rutherford, NJ 07073
(201) 460–4022

NORTH CAROLINA SPORTS
HALL OF FAME
3509 Haworth Drive
Raleigh, NC 28510
(919) 781–4774

PRINCE EDWARD ISLAND
SPORTS HALL OF FAME
42 Newland Crescent
Charlottestown, P.E.I., Canada
C1A 4H7
(902) 436–3658

P.G.A. GOLF HALL OF FAME
P.O. Box 12458
Palm Beach Gardens, FL 33410
(305) 626–3600

PRO FOOTBALL HALL OF FAME
2121 George Hallas Dr. N.W.
Canton, OH 44708
(216) 456–8207

ST. LOUIS SPORTS HALL OF
FAME, INC.
100 Stadium Plaza
St. Louis, MO 63102
(314) 421–6790

SAN DIEGO HALL OF
CHAMPIONS, INC.
1439 El Prado
Balboa Park
San Diego, CA 92101
(714) 234–2544

SASKATCHEWAN SPORTS HALL
OF FAME
2205 Victoria Avenue
Regina, Saskatchewan, Canada
S4P 0S4
(306) 522–3651

SPORT NOVA SCOTIA HALL OF
FAME
P.O. Box 3010 S.
Halifax, Nova Scotia, Canada
B3J 3G6
(902) 425–5450

SPORTS HALL OF FAME OF
MAINE
Apt. 148, Promenade East
Portland, ME 04101
(207) 772–0682

STATE OF MICHIGAN SPORTS
HALL OF FAME
1010 Joanne Court
Bloomfield Hills, MI 48013
(313) 646–2216

TEXAS SPORTS HALL OF FAME
FOUNDATION
601 Fidelity Union Life Blvd.
Dallas, TX 75201
(214) 871–2844

TEXAS SPORTS HALL OF
CHAMPIONS AND TEXAS
TENNIS MUSEUM
P.O. Box 3475
Waco, TX 75707
(817) 756–2307

TROTTING HORSE MUSEUM
AND HALL OF FAME
P.O. Box 590
Goshen, NY 10924
(914) 294–6330

UNITED STATES FIGURE
SKATING ASSOCIATION
HALL OF FAME
20 First Street
Colorado Springs, CO 80906
(303) 625–5200

UNITED STATES GOLF ASSN.
HALL OF FAME
Golf House
Far Hills, NJ 07931
(201) 234–2300

UNITED STATES HOCKEY HALL
OF FAME, INC.
P.O. Box 657
Eveleth, MN 55734
(218) 749–5167

UNITED STATES OLYMPIC
COMMITTEE
1750 East Boulder Street
Colorado Springs, CO 80909
(303) 632–5551

UNITED STATES TRACK &
HALL OF FAME
P.O. Box 297
Angola, IN 46703
(219) 495–7735

VETERANS PARK DISTRICT
SPORTS MUSEUM
1201 N. 24th Street
Melrose Park, IL 60160
(312) 343–5151

VOLLEYBALL HALL OF FAME
P.O. Box 1895
444 Dwight Street
Holyoke, MA 01040
(413) 536–5770

WORLD GOLF HALL OF FAME
P.O. Box 1908
Pinehurst, NC 28374
(919) 295–6651

APPENDIX D

MAGAZINES AND NEWSPAPERS

American Sports. P.O. Box 6100, Rosemead, CA 91770.

Athletic Administration. 24651 Detroit Road, Cleveland, OH 44115.

Athletic Business. 1842 Hoffman Street, Suite 201, Madison, WI 53704.

Athletic Director and Coach. 450 Lafayette Street, Salem, MA 01970.

Athletic Journal. 1719 Howard Street, Evanston, IL 60202.

Basketball News. 114 Madison Avenue, Coral Gables, FL 33134.

Basketball Weekly. 19830 Mack Avenue, Grosse Pointe, MI 48236.

Bicycling. 119 Paul Drive, San Rafael, CA 94903.

Black Sports. 31 East 28th Street, New York, NY 10016.

Boating. P.O. Box 2773, Boulder, CO 80302.

Canadian Old Timers Sports News. Box 951, Peterborough, Ont., Canada K9J 7A5.

City Sports. P.O. Box 3693, San Francisco, CA 94119.

Football News. 19830 Mack Avenue, Grosse Pointe, MI 48236.

Hot Rod Magazine. Peterson Publishing Co., 5959 Hollywood Blvd., Los Angeles, CA 90028.

Inside Sports. 990 Grove Street, Evanston, IL 60201.

Journal of Sport Management. Box 5076, Champaign, IL 61825.

JUCO Review. P.O. Box 7305, Colorado Springs, CO 80933.

Karate Illustrated. 1847 W. Empire Avenue, Burbank, CA 90504.

Motor Trend Magazine. Peterson Publishing Co., 5959 Hollywood Blvd., Los Angeles, CA 90028.

National Coach. 3423 E. Silver Springs Blvd. S–9, Ocala, FL 32670.

NAIA News. 1221 Baltimore Avenue, Kansas City, MO 64105.

NCAA News. 6201 College Blvd., Overland Park, KS 66211.

The Olympian. P.O. Box 1699, Colorado Springs, CO 80901–9938.

The Physician and Sports Medicine. 4530 W. 77th Street, Suite 350, Minneapolis, MN 55435.

Scholastic Coach. Scholastic Coach, Inc., 730 Broadway, New York, NY 10033.

Skin Diver. Peterson Publishing Co., 5959 Hollywood Blvd., Los Angeles, CA 90028.

Sport. McFadden-Bartell Corporation, 205 E. 42nd St., New York, NY 10017.

Sporting News. 1212 North Lindenbergh, St. Louis, MO 63166.

Sports Illustrated. 1271 Avenue of the Americas, New York, NY 10021.

Sports Woman. 119 Paul Drive, Rafael, CA 94903.

Swimming World. Swimming World, Inc., 8622 Bellanca, Los Angeles, CA 90045.

Track and Field News. 2570 El Camino Real, Suite 606, Mountain View, CA 94040.

Women Sports. Women's Sport Publishing Company, 1660 S. Amphlet Blvd., San Mateo, CA 50306.

Women's Sports and Fitness. 1919 14th Street, Suite 421, Boulder, CO 80302.

Women's Sports Pages. P.O. Box 151534, Chevy Chase, MD 20825.

World Tennis. 3 Park Avenue, New York, NY 10036.